Happy Families

An imaginative sampler, made in the reign of George IV, almost
certainly a portrait of Kate Barlow's home. 19th century.
Photograph by Studio Wreford.

Happy Families

Growing Up in the Eighteenth and Nineteenth Centuries

Jean Latham

ADAM & CHARLES BLACK · LONDON

First published 1974
by A & C Black Ltd
4 5 and 6 Soho Square
London WIV 6AD

© 1974 Jean Latham

ISBN 0 7136 1442 0

Filmset by Photoprint Plates Ltd, Rayleigh, Essex
and Printed in Great Britain by BAS Printers Limited, Wallop, Hampshire

Contents

Acknowledgements

Grateful thanks to Mary Livie-Noble for typing and helpful suggestions, to Llewellyn Robins for photographing my collection, and to Jennifer May for her contribution, as well as to Rupert Gentle for photographs from his own possessions. Also, I would like to acknowledge help from Marlborough Public Library in procuring books for research, and to the authors of the books in my Bibliography whose work was so valuable to me.

Special thanks to Belinda Peacey for lending me her own notes about the Yong Roscius and to Michael O'Regan for the family papers he let me see about his illustrious ancestor, William Rowan Hamilton. Also to Sylvia Townsend-Warner for her great grandmother's memoirs.

Jean Latham,
Marlborough, 1973

Illustrations

Foreword

Here is a book about children, some famous and some obscure. It is necessarily incomplete, but it is meant as an appetiser to encourage curiosity and to inspire readers to follow up the subjects of their own inclinations.

Clues can be found in antiques and bygones of the period which enlighten the written word. Visits to museums are also very stimulating, as well as stately homes.

Although the book has not been prepared in haste, but written for pleasure and hoping to give pleasure to others, I cannot hope that it will be completely free from errors. Forgive its shortcomings and suspend harsh judgements please, and read it for enjoyment.

Jean Latham
Marlborough, 1973

CHAPTER ONE

Beginnings

Starting to write a book about children's lives in the past two or three hundred years seemed a small enough canvas to work on at first sight. Children's lives have brief records. We will divide the story into five or six parts, thinks the author, and then divide each part into chapters. Like any other project, the less you know about it the less there is to choose from; the more you read the more difficult it is to make a choice. That slim, manageable volume begins to swell menacingly into a huge tome. Each chapter, bursting at its seams, could easily be expanded into a book.

Novelists often comment with satisfaction on the way their characters seem to take over the plot and their books are, to all intents and purposes, written by the *dramatis personae*. The work of a non-fiction writer is largely a matter of selection; and like Frank Churchill in *Emma*, 'sometimes one conjectures right, and sometimes one conjectures wrong . . . ' about the salient facts to be left in or left out. Obviously everybody's tastes cannot be catered for, and those reading this book in expectation of a recital of dynasties, records and a disciplined study of historical research must look elsewhere. We are here concerned with the story of children and their simple human joys and sometimes sufferings; their small triumphs and disasters; their games, learning, apparel, food and everyday lives. We look at the royal, the middling, the poor, the gifted and the average child.

It would have been tempting to span the centuries and explore the world of Chaucer's 'heepe' of children who 'learned in the schole year by year . . . to singen and to read'; and a little later to consider John Lydgate's *The Babees' Book*, with its rules for good behaviour. In his childhood Lydgate chose to play with cherry-stones instead of going to school and he ran about 'like a young colt without a bridle'. The ABC used to be learnt from a horn book, a printed sheet cased in transparent horn. Shakespeare would have learnt his letters from one when he was, 'with his satchel, and shining morning face, creeping like snail unwillingly to school'.

what I can to keep thee from falling into everlasting fire'. To cheer up the recipient of his letter this writer includes a story about a boy 'who had a comfortable death when he was 12'.

What a mercy that the change of attitude towards children to a kinder and gentler outlook gradually lightened their lives. To be sure, Freud re-discovered the hidden monster in them, but instead of birching them parents now sent them to a doctor to be 'analysed' and sometimes even went themselves for the same treatment.

Let us now dip into the past and see if children have changed very much in essentials. After all, the maddening old *cliché* about the child being father to the man is probably true enough. Mankind, they say, has not altered very much through the centuries. Or has he?

THE PRIVILEGED

Boys and girls of medieval times were sent to be pages or maids at the age of nine or ten in great houses to learn good manners. Presumably their parents preferred to get rid of them, since although babies might be cherished, toddlers were a nuisance; and as for the eight and ten year olds, well, everyone hoped that they would grow up as soon as possible. Children were then taught to kneel to receive their parents' blessings and to stand in their presence and call them 'Sir' and 'Madam'. In fact they were not considered as personalities so much as chattels belonging to the parents.

In the eighteenth century, however, children spent much more time at home, albeit mostly in the nursery. This was chiefly because the large families could be more easily managed in a separate establishment and they would be less likely to cause inconvenience and irritation to the adults of the family. As Dr Johnson observed drily, 'Boarding Schools were established for the conjugal quiet of the parents'.

In Victorian days everything was centred round the home and domestic life. Travelling was made *en famille* for long periods, wintering in a villa in Pau or even Florence or Rome; in the summer, taking lodgings at the seaside. Parties were quite an addiction and, instead of watching television, round games were played or musical evenings took place. Father read aloud some evenings whilst mama and the daughters quietly employed their fingers with needlework and other crafts. The younger children in starched frocks came downstairs and sat or played for half an hour very quietly, after their tea in the nursery. On Sundays they were allowed only to play with the Noah's ark and read the Bible.

4

A Victorian doll's room boxed in a frame, the background of cut-out paper made specially for the purpose. The walls are covered with contemporary prints, drawings and silhouettes in home-made frames. A parlour pastime, useless but decorative. Photograph by Studio Wreford.

The houses of the middle and upper classes had to be large to lodge the huge families. There was a room for every conceivable activity. The morning- or breakfast-room also accommodated the lady of the house when she wrote her letters or planned the menus. Father's study might combine with a smoking-room for men visitors. The drawing-room and dining-room were big and full of furniture and there might also be a library and a billiard-room. There would probably be a school-room where the governess taught the older children as well as a nursery for the toddlers. Bedrooms, of course, were numerous, and in a separate wing were the servants' quarters comprising a huge kitchen, scullery, still-room, laundry in all probability, and a servants' hall. In the most inconvenient part of the house, the attics, there were bedrooms for the staff. The children would be as segregated from the social life of the household as the servants and indeed the happiest part of their days were usually spent in the kitchen or the garden.

5

Of course, where the upper classes led the way, the middling ones followed the fashion and social distinctions grew into many sub-divisions and groups. Ever since the seventeenth century clergymen were steadily increasing in importance and by Regency times they were often the younger sons of county families, like Henry Tilney in Jane Austen's *Northanger Abbey* or Edmund Bertram in *Mansfield Park*. Clerical life is rich in literary associations. We have only to think of the Brontës and their home in Haworth Parsonage, of Trollope and of Mrs Ewing for a start.

Jane Eyre was written in the 1840s, as we shall see when we discuss governesses. Jane, still almost a child, enters Thornfield and describes a drawing-room of early Victorian taste, where the red Bohemian glass on the 'pale Parian mantelpiece' is reflected in the long pier glasses, a 'general blending of snow and fire'. The carpet too was white on which seemed laid garlands of flowers. The couches and ottomans were crimson. Jane, as we remember, had come to be governess to little Adèle, who was always dressed in Parisian silks of rose colour or blue.

Dickens describes comfort and cosiness, slightly lower in the social scale. In *Great Expectations* Mr Wemmick and the Aged Parent live in 'the smallest house I ever saw; with the queerest gothic windows (by far the greater part of them sham) and a gothic door almost too small to get in at'. *Bleak House,* by contrast, is 'one of those delightfully irregular houses where you go up and down steps out of one room into another' full of odd little passages and corners and not at all bleak. It is full of warmth, too, and friendliness, with crayon portraits, a needlework sampler of an alphabet, fruit and a kettle and flowers decorating the wallpaper, the curtains and the carpets. Another establishment is again different. The Snagsbys live in Chancery Lane and the little maid-of-all-work, probably twelve or younger, regards this dreary home as 'a Temple of plenty and splendour. She believes the little drawing-room upstairs, always kept, as one may say, with its hair in papers and its pinafore on, to be the most elegant apartment in Christendom'. The poor little workhouse waif helps to clean and polish this room, helps to lay out the best tea-service for the Snagsbys and their detestable friends the Chadbands, and helps to spread the table with 'dainty new bread, crusty twists, cool fresh butter, thin slices of ham, tongue and German sausage, and delicate little rows of anchovies nestling in parsley; not to mention new-laid eggs to be brought up warm in a napkin and hot buttered toast'. The little maid will never get so much as a crumb of this appetising high-tea.

Another Dickensian home is Boffin's Bower in *Our Mutual Friend*, Mrs Boffin being 'a highflyer at fashion' who furnished her parlour with a flower-laden carpet, a sofa complete with sofa-table and footstool and stuffed birds and waxed fruit under glass shades. The oddest thing about the room was the arrangements Mr Boffin had designed to suit his own taste; a luxurious amateur tap-room with a wooden settle and table on each side of the fire and even a sanded floor. Surely this strange arrangement, with the array of bottles and glasses on one of the tables, must have had its counter-part in real life which Dickens saw as a boy and later immortalised.

Who, nowadays, reads Grossmith's *Diary of a Nobody*? Here the Pooters live in a six-room house with a basement near a railway station and we find that by the 1890s the aesthetic movement has reached suburbia. Carrie Pooter has adorned the tinted family photographs with bows of Liberty silk and her husband

Lady Rushout and her children by T. Watson. This is a mezzotint (first state of three) *c* 1800. Courtesy of Sotheby's.

celebrates a small rise in his salary, as a clerk, by allowing her to buy a chimney-glass for the best parlour.

The end of the nineteenth century saw a cutting-down in the size of families, though this happened in the homes most able to support large ones, the upper and professional classes and the tradesmen and craftsmen. The poorer families continued to produce ten to twelve children. What was different in the outlook of people then was their attitude to the badly off. They believed that poverty was just something that happened to some people and could not be cured, only helped by the philanthropic 'better-off', who provided soup, bread, vegetables and meat at their own expense.

Children in the middle and upper classes were, of course, generally brought up by nurses and governesses, who were themselves given plenty of help from under-nurses and nursery-maids. On the whole they were kind and much loved by their charges and indeed remained sometimes with one family all their lives, taking care of a second generation of babies and eventually living on the premises in a bed-sitter in happy retirement, surrounded by the only family they knew.

Nannies are now comparatively rare and sitters-in have taken their place. Sixty years ago they were still quite numerous and in a large household there might be a staff of twenty. The children would then have been given a head nurse, under-nurse, a nursery-maid and a house-maid to look after them all. Nursery fires had to be lit by 6 o'clock and the head nurse was woken by a housemaid at half past seven with a cup of tea and some thin bread and butter. Nursery breakfast was about 8 o'clock, and by 10 o'clock the prams were being pushed out for the first airing of the day. At 1 o'clock it was lunch time and then another walk and at 4 o'clock tea time. The only time the children saw their parents was the hour between tea and bedtime when they presented themselves in immaculate clothes and corkscrew curls and might be asked to recite *How Doth the Little Busy Bee*, or *The Boy Stood on the Burning Deck* or some other suitable poetry learnt in the schoolroom.

The nursery-maids took their first place at fourteen and in 1900 they would be earning ten pounds a year plus keep. The nursery-maid was on the very lowest social rung of the ladder of the staff in a big house and she had meals with the under-nurse in the day nursery, whilst the head nurse had the amusement of dining in the housekeeper's room and meeting valets and ladies' maids who had come to the house on a visit. The nursery-maid could sometimes work her way up to the position of head nurse and, as the children were generally under strict discipline and very amenable, it was a physically exacting but not mentally exhausting job.

The endless changing of the children's clothes took up a lot of time. For instance, no self-respecting nurse allowed her charge

Fairy Tales (dated 1870) by George G. Kilburne. This was exhibited at the Royal Academy in 1872. Courtesy of Sotheby's.

to wear the same clothes mornings and afternoons. Then the visit to the drawing-room necessitated yet another change, and the nursery staff were kept busy washing and ironing sashes and muslin frocks. The boys wore velvet knickers with frilled silk blouses.

The 1900 period nurseries always had a doll's house and a rocking-horse amongst the toys, and sometimes a screen decorated with cut-out pictures and old greetings cards, probably made by Grand-mama when young. Another essential was the damask table-cloths and the nursery plates decorated with Peter Rabbit or the Florence Upton golliwogs or perhaps earlier still survivals from Mama's youth. Everybody had been taught to be so careful of their own and other people's property that breakages and wastage were very rare. Children's toys and tableware of the past are not hard to come by now.

Does it sound dull to have been brought up in one of those Victorian or Edwardian upper-class nurseries? In fact there was quite a lot of fun, what with Papa coming up to play rather noisily with his children and, in the way fathers have, exciting them to romps nobody else allowed. Then there were parties and visits to friends, learning to ride and to dance, magic-lantern and con-juring shows on birthdays and visits to the seaside. Most children could read by the time they were five and tinkle away easy exercises on the piano. Those living in the country had plenty to do in their own big gardens with pets to look after, helping the gardener to feed the horses and poultry, collecting the eggs and, perhaps, messing about with tadpoles and newts in the pond. True, they were invariably accompanied by a nurse or other adult to see they neither endangered themselves nor became covered in grime; but, just as the cottage children did not miss the constant super-vision and care they had never known, nor did these upper class children miss the freedom they had not yet experienced. Soon enough they would be pitchforked into the world of school and the tender mercies of their own generation and that was certainly not a sheltered life.

THE UNDER-PRIVILEGED

In the back streets the children led very different lives. In the nineteenth century there was no unemployment pay, no old age pension, and health and unemployment insurance only came into force in 1911. The shadow of the dreaded work-house hung over the old people as these resorts were not only soulless places but it was considered to be a disgrace to have to go there. Most children left school at twelve, even in 1900, but in 1902 primary and second-ary education started and State Board schools were abolished. From then on any child clever enough could go to the university and no career was closed to anybody.

To be sure the new schools were not ideal, but they did teach well. The children from huge families could not afford new clothes but cut down and contrived dresses and pinafores; trousers and jackets from older brothers and sisters were stitched by the ever-busy mothers, and pinafores were the nearest to a uniform they had. Certainly cleanliness was a problem for poor families then and one teacher in Hoxton, in pre-first World War days, remembered the fleas and bugs and ringworm, eye-troubles and impetigo from which her pupils suffered. As early as 1909 there were school meals, and the Salvation Army distributed one-farthing tickets to the really needy ones for breakfast, which consisted of a cup of cocoa and a large piece of bread and dripping. If the teachers heard children could not afford new boots or shoes they organised methods to supply these. Some of the children worked for a pittance both before and after attending school each day. That must have been very tiring, but of course, even today, children are ready to earn something by doing the 'paper round'. The only difference is that today they keep their earnings whereas in the nineteenth century and the turn of the twentieth century they gave their earnings towards the feeding of their families.

Still, the schools provided fun as well as work. Games, dancing and acting were entered into with great gusto out of school hours and the children even learnt to play the violin, at sixpence a lesson, and joined in school concerts. In fact, it was largely the school teachers who planned and contrived to make the children's lives exciting and worthwhile out of as well as in school, and they knew the backgrounds of the children too and took a genuine interest in their welfare.

This was an enormous improvement on earlier times. In the eighteenth century anyone could exploit children, and many did so. A parish in London, for instance, kept a Lancashire Mill stocked with child labour, probably between the ages of five and seven, stipulating only that the Mill must receive one mentally retarded child in every 20 provided. These wretched children worked for at least 14 hours a day and sometimes as much as 18 hours. Lord Shaftesbury, as late as 1842, publicised the horrifying facts about children of three and four working in mines, and infants on all fours dragging coal carts along which they had fastened by chains around their waists. Not until 1887 was an Act passed forbidding

11

The Meeting of the Haves and the Have-nots. An anonymous print published by Laurie and Whittle in London in 1794. Photograph by Studio Wreford.

boys under twelve and women and girls of whatever age they might be to work below ground in mines.

All the same it was impossible to keep a check on everybody, and many a back street continued to supply child labour in defiance of the law. On the other hand, remarkably enough, there were many who were ready to testify to the happiness they found in work that today we are horrified to contemplate. One girl working in a Glasgow factory ended her account by saying that despite the terrible things she saw of people starving and crawling with lice, she was

Mid Victorian life for the poor. *Punch*, as usual, holds up a mirror to all classes of society. The drawing is by John Leech. Photograph by Studio Wreford.

happy and perfectly content with her lot. Another boy, of the same period, remembered how his mother told him about her days as a child slave, but her unquenchable spirit of gaiety and courage fought through to give her own family of nine, out of which seven were boys, a poor but cheerful and happy home life. The son started work in 1896, when he was twelve, down a mine with his father, sometimes spending 31 hours on end underground. Still he found time to earn extra as a butcher's roundsman, bringing home a pound of sausages and a shilling to his proud and delighted mother.

Even so they had time to enjoy themselves and went to the travelling theatres and to the circus, the children getting a free pass for themselves by going round with handbills.

Just as many people still believe that cats must not be fed or else they won't catch the mice and rats, so one Georgian wrote that 'the lower classes must be kept poor or they will never be industrious'. Poverty and crime were almost synonymous words, so it is difficult to square that remark with the rising crime rate which was the direct result of poverty. Against this, in fairness to the Georgians, we must remember that from the rather smug and contented middle class sprang a truly humanitarian attitude and a growing interest in philanthropy. Self-righteous, moralising they might be, but they were instrumental in setting up many reforms. They battled against the slave trade, set up the Marine Society and Charity Schools and the Foundling Hospital. We might as well remember here that the Victorians did not invent what they are often accused of fostering, that is 'sweated labour'. Could it have been the 'polite' age of the eighteenth century from which it was inherited?

Now the Evangelical bourgeoisie, in fact, was on its way towards becoming the dominant, if not ruling, class. All of a sudden cleanliness was being considered next to godliness in respectability, and religion and orderliness the rule to be observed. Nevertheless, conditions for the poor both in town and country were still very, very bad.

In 1839 the annual death toll was double that suffered by all the allied armies at Waterloo. The Poor Law and sanitary officials presented a report to the Home Secretary in 1842 on *The Sanitary Condition of the Labouring Population*. They were mainly concerned with rural homes. One doctor noted that a horse stood behind the bed and fowls roosted on the bedposts. There were at least ten people in this hovel, and usually the cottages had only two rooms. Often three or four families would inhabit the same home. Incidentally, this was the year that income tax began as a permanent thorn in everybody's flesh. No laws were passed to help the conditions of the rural population after the Report, but Prince Albert interested himself in problems of sanitation. It was, in fact, nearly as bad in rich and royal homes. A new lavatory at Buckingham Palace above the Queen's bedroom, for instance, drained out over the leads in front of her dressing-room, and the Prince Consort himself was suspected to have caught the typhus that killed him from defective cesspools at Windsor Castle.

In contrast to the romantic hovels in which the labourers lived, there were 'cottages of gentility' dating as early as the eighteenth century. We have only to look at Jane Austen's novels. The Dashwoods lived in Barton Cottage, which had four principal bedrooms and two garrets with a sitting-room sixteen feet square. A cottage in this sense of the word is, of course, a misnomer. In the sixteenth and seventeenth centuries cottage simply meant a one-room shack with a roof of reeds or a timber construction filled in with mud. The oak-beamed cottages that have survived until today were not originally for the poor man but were made by prosperous farmers, tradesmen or merchants for themselves.

By the eighteenth century although the rich were now living in those delightful red brick or stone houses with pillared porticos of Palladian design and symmetrical sash-windows, the labourers still called home a one-room outdated hovel. Amazingly enough, foreign visitors were nevertheless surprised at our cottagers' good diet as compared with their own.

Supper Time: a cottage interior, nineteenth century, by Bernard Pothast. Courtesy of Sotheby's.

Oliver Goldsmith's vicar of Wakefield lived in a one-storey cottage with a thatched roof. It housed his wife and their six children and himself. They had no complaints, apparently, but perhaps that was poetic licence. Some poets and amateur artists were much inspired by the romance of love in a cottage, however dark, dirty and evil-smelling it might be in wretched reality. Crabbe, at least, had the common sense to write, 'Where plenty smiles, alas! She smiles for few'. He was not affected by the cult for the picturesque.

By 1815 the plight of the poor was bad indeed. The end of war brought unemployment with the armed forces swelling the numbers by something near half a million. As for Scotland, their living conditions were atrocious. The peasants shared their roof with their livestock; horses, pigs, chickens, dogs and cats. The one bedroom was usually a loft, if they had one. Even Crabbe, in spite of having seen such miserable, unhappy homes, was able to write of the 'humble tradesmen in their evening glee'. So let's hope the picture was not always and entirely despairing, unlit by any joy.

Much later, from the secure background of upper middle class comparative wealth, Hilaire Belloc was writing his delightful Cautionary Tales to amuse both children and their parents of the 1890s and onwards.

> 'Your little hands were made to take
> The better things and leave the worse ones:
> They also may be used to shake
> The massive paws of elder persons'.

By this time the national conscience was wide awake to the horrors of poverty and child labour and better times were coming, so they hoped.

In the coming chapters we will look at the lives of children in many different situations; rich and poor, gifted and ordinary, good, bad and indifferent. We might begin, by way of an appetiser, with the most unusual of all, the child prodigies.

CHAPTER TWO

Infant Prodigies

Looking back into history we find that certain children seem to have been precocious in every respect so that it is difficult to draw the line between clever children with every opportunity to learn early and the *Oxford Dictionary's* definition of a prodigy, 'an extraordinary, astonishing person'. In German they call such children 'wunderkinder', when they show early signs of genius or ability along certain lines. Who can we find to qualify? Dante fell in love with Beatrice when they were both only nine years old, John Evelyn mentions Lord Arlington's daughter as being 'the sweetest, hopefullest, most beautiful child,' who, not in the least to the Diarist's surprise, was married at the age of five to a 'rudely bred' bridegroom of nine years old. Evelyn's own son read English, Latin and French at the age of two-and-a-half. Here surely is a prodigy candidate. Thomas Lawrence was painting portraits when he was seven. Anna Seward, the Swan of Lichfield, who bequeathed her poetry to Sir Walter Scott*, and met Boswell and Dr Johnson after, recited with remarkable verve and enjoyment Milton's *L'Allegro* and *Il Penseroso* at the age of three. Did she really understand it then or only speak it like a parrot? Princess Charlotte of Wales was declaiming a less exalted poem when she was three, 'How doth the little busy bee . . .'. This we know from the admiring Hannah More. Probably the champion of precocious remarks came from Macaulay whose mother reported that on noticing her irritation, when he was a very small boy, he commented, 'Madam, it is part of that vast scheme of annoyance which governs this sublunacy (sic) sphere'.

Arithmetical prodigies, who excel at chess and produce lightning quick calculations have remarkable memories for figures and visual or auditory imagery; but they are seldom much good at anything else. The most common prodigy is the musical one; far less common is a precocious ability in acting, painting, drawing and writing. Albrecht Dürer painted a self portrait when he was thirteen. Pascal was secretly inventing his own type of geometry

*He published it in 1810 with a memoir.

when he was eleven. We have to remember that of these children, who are both born and made, with the quality of exceptionally retentive memory and a capacity for relating and organising experiences, few of the mental prodigies we know about in history, with the exception of music, seem to have met early expectations. Early musical genius, on the other hand, rarely seems to have faded into oblivion.

Another point to note is that all the outstanding original geniuses who have achieved fame could no doubt have been identified in their extreme youth. Precocious behaviour is invariably noticed. Bishop Thirlwall, born in 1797, can be compared with John Stuart Mill, who died in 1873. The Bishop, like Mill, read Latin at three and Greek at four; when he was eleven a volume of his 'verses, moral tales and sermons' was published. It received favourable notices from the critics. The Bishop was later on a friend of such delightful men as Monckton Milnes, Tennyson, Hallam and Lord Melbourne. He loved children and animals. A legendary story goes that he was always in later years accompanied by a large dog trained to recognise and bite curates. Gladstone certainly thought well of this gifted child when he became a man, describing him as 'one of the most masculine, powerful and luminous intellects that have for generations been known among the Bishops of England'.

The musical prodigies are numerous. Besides Mozart, whom we shall take as an outstanding example, there were Schubert and Mendelssohn, both of whom composed before they were twelve; Chopin, who played in public aged nine; Richard Strauss, who composed a polka and a song when he was six; Richard Wagner, who wrote a grand tragedy when he was fourteen; and Franz Liszt, who performed in public at the age of nine. There are others as well. Beethoven himself composed when he was ten and appeared in a concert aged eight, as well as becoming a chapel organist at eleven and conducting the Opera band at rehearsals when he was twelve. Haydn tells his own story about his early promise. 'By the time I was six', he wrote, 'I stood up like a man and sang masses in the church choir and could play a little on the clavier and violin'. Genius certainly does make its mark young. Mozart heard Beethoven, fourteen years his junior, improvise on a theme, and he prophesied, 'pay attention to him, he will make a noise in the world some day'.

Acting brilliance is probably the commonest amongst children, particularly with those born, so to speak, on the stage. We will notice this when we meet young William Betty later on. The best known fictional prodigy was the one that Dickens based on a real life child in his *Nicholas Nickleby*. Mr Vincent Crummles was the actor-manager of a company in Portsmouth which Nicholas and Smike joined after their flight from Dotheboys Hall. He himself was a bit of a prodigy, since he had played 'the heavy children' in a travelling theatre, when he was eighteen months old. His daughter, however, known as the Infant Phenomenon, was his pride and joy, who first appeared before the astonished Nicholas dressed in 'a dirty white frock with two tucks up to the knees . . . pink gauze bonnet, green veil and curl-papers' in the act named *The Indian Savage and the Maiden*. There was considerable doubt in the minds of the rest of the company as to her right to the title of Infant, as they had seen her billed as ten years old for five seasons at least.

The true-life counterpart of Crummles is believed to have been Thomas Donald Davenport (1792–1851)* and his daughter Jean certainly did appear at the age of eight years old playing Richard III. The family toured the United States in 1838 and this Infant Phenomenon was made to play highly unsuitable parts like Shylock and Sir Peter Teazle, which nevertheless seem to have been a great success.

Selecting our prodigies is a matter of personal taste up to a point, as there were many of them, particularly in the nineteenth century. Let us begin with a famous and tragic child who was a poet.

THOMAS CHATTERTON
1752–1770

'I thought of Chatterton, the Marvellous Boy', wrote Wordsworth in 1802†, some thirty years after the ill-starred poet's death. Thomas Chatterton was the posthumous son of a writing-master. His father was unusually intelligent, being interested in music and poetry, the occult sciences and collecting antique coins, besides having a good knowledge of academic subjects. He was also a lay clerk of Bristol Cathedral. Nobody, I believe, has ever said that he would have been a good parent. He died before his gifted son was born, leaving a 20-year-old wife practically penniless, with a little daughter and the expected baby. Mrs Chatterton went to live with her mother-in-law and took up sewing to earn a pittance towards bringing up her two children.

Unlike the average prodigy, if such a paradox exists, Chatterton was a difficult child. At first he was regarded as unteachable at the Dame School to which he was sent. However, his sister taught him

*See *Oxford Companion to the Theatre*.
†*Resolution and Independence*.

19

to read and soon he was reading books about music and metaphysics, astronomy, heraldry and mathematics. Apparently his greatest pleasure was to study the beautiful illuminated capitals in an old book of music that had belonged to his father. At eight years old he was sent to a Charity school called Colston's Hospital as a boarder. We can picture him wearing the medieval blue coat and yellow stockings which was the school's uniform. He may well have then begun to see himself as 'the good priest Thomas Rowley' whose poems he invented later on, saying that they had been found amongst documents in St Mary's, Redcliffe at Bristol. He had always lived near this church and spent a lot of time in his early childhood soaking in its gothic charms, so that gradually his affection for the church developed into a passion. He rescued old records, which his father had been given from the church's muniments room, saving them from his mother's uncaring hands. She was using them as spills to light her fire. Up he carried his treasures to his refuge in the attic and there he spent hours with them and with his pen and ink, paints and charcoal.

The first poem Chatterton wrote, as far as anyone knows, was published in a Bristol paper when he was ten and in 1764 he wrote an excellent satire called *Apostate Will* and some other verses.

At fourteen he left school for an attorney's office, where he was apprenticed and was expected to spend his time copying out legal papers. However mechanical and dull the work might be, at least it was not arduous, so Chatterton worked away on his poems. Most of them at this time, unfortunately for posterity, were destroyed angrily by his employer. We can hardly blame the poor man. This boy, so difficult and proud and uncompromising, can have had little in common with most of the people with whom he rubbed shoulders. Perhaps his mother had brought him up to revere the memory of his father. Certainly he shared his father's interest in the occult and sometimes he sat up late at night trying to raise spirits with the aid of a book about magic.

Odd though he must have seemed to the average teenager, he consorted with a group of friends of 15 and 16 years old, most of whom were apprenticed to some trade. They used to meet and discuss, rather arrogantly, matters of politics and literature and, as our modern speech has it, to chat up the local girls. Behind these normal occupations, however, Chatterton was living in an imaginative world of his own, obsessed by a deep interest in the past and driven by his remarkable poetic genius.

In 1768, when he was sixteen, there was a grand opening of the new bridge at Bristol and Chatterton was given a part in the ceremony. He produced a pseudo-archaic document of his own devising which purported to describe in medieval language the original opening of the old thirteenth century bridge. A Bristol newspaper published the report. This must have been the turning point when the boy, perhaps afraid to reveal his secret to an unsympathetic world, insisted that the transcript was one of those his father had been given from the Church of St Mary. So in 1768 was born the imaginary poet Thomas Rowley, a fifteenth century monk and a friend, said Chatterton, of an authentic historical character called William Canynge, a Bristol merchant. Once embarked on his elaborate deception there was no retreat. He fabricated pedigrees, poems and other documents, claiming that he had the originals. He gave his secular monk a patron, the Bristol merchant Canynge, whom Chatterton said had endowed the poet Rowley with great munificence. He added, for better measure, that Rowley indeed rivalled Chaucer and of course, since Canynge was an historical personage, there was his effigy for all to see lying in St Mary's Church. Three dupes swallowed the young poet's story whole. One was William Barrett, an antiquarian-minded surgeon who was writing a history of Bristol; another was a man called George Symes Calcott noted for his eccentricity. He used to wear a ring in mourning for the long-dead Charles I. He also preserved a box containing all his own teeth, which his executors were instructed to 'put in the coffin when I die'. Presumably this was so that he might give the Almighty as little trouble as possible when re-assembling him on the Last Day. The third dupe was a pewterer called Henry Burgum. Calcott was the man to whom Chatterton first showed his poems. One of them had been written when he was only 11 years old, according to the testimony of a school friend to whom he showed 'Elinoure and Juga' in 1764. The publisher Dodsley included it in the *Town and Country Magazine* of 1769 and in fact this, sadly, was the only 'Rowley' poem to be published in Chatterton's lifetime.

The young poet had certainly not browsed in vain amongst his father's faded parchments and other historical books. He culled names from the churchyard to give authenticity to his alter ego Rowley, and he even added learned footnotes to the poems.

What a fascinating Walter Mitty life this 'marvellous boy' led, with the thriving, noisy, boisterous city life of eighteenth century Bristol pulsating round him. What a source of inner comfort and inspiration his imaginary poet must have been to him. He had a great disappointment, however, the first of so many others, when he ventured to write to Horace Walpole, enclosing 'a curious manuscript', a history of painting in England, supposed to be by Rowley. Walpole appears to have been taken in at first and replied with an encouraging and courteous letter. Poor Chatterton then made the mistake of sending more samples of his poems, adding with touching naïveté details about himself and his circumstances. He longed desperately for a patron like the one he had invented for his 'Thomas Rowley'. Walpole had supposed his correspondent to be a venerable antiquarian and the boy's letter made him suspect that he was dealing with an unscrupulous apprentice trying out his luck. Thomas Gray, to whom Walpole sent the poems for his opinion, replied with the verdict that they were forgeries. Walpole then wrote a friendly letter advising the boy to carry on with his apprenticeship and to look after his mother. What a cruel blow this was to the ambitious young poet. How was he to know that Walpole was already smarting from the fairly recent embarrassment of having backed Macpherson's bogus 'Ossian', which Dr Johnson so thunderingly denounced? '. . . What would you have me retract,' he wrote to Macpherson, 'I thought your book an imposture; I think it an imposture still'. This letter, by the way, is often said to be the rudest one in the English language.

Chatterton was bitterly disillusioned. He believed, quite wrongly, that he was spurned on account of his youth and his humble birth. As usual he took refuge in poetry and wrote:

> 'Walpole, I thought not I should ever see
> So mean a Heart as thine has proved to be'.

Although he did not send this poem to Walpole, his letter showed how hurt he was. 'Though I am but 16 years of age,' he wrote, 'I have lived long enough to see that poverty attends literature'.

Poor Horace Walpole has been given by posterity the unenviable rôle of the man who caused the boy-poet's suicide. He assured everybody that he was blameless. 'I am as innocent of the death of Julius Caesar' he cried. But the mud has stuck ever since. We might just as well blame William Beckford for dying before he could make good his promise to Chatterton that he would print the young poet's second letter praising Beckford's successful tenure of the office of Lord Mayor of London. Desolated at another prospective patron's loss, the 17 year-old penniless young man took this luckless letter of praise and wrote on the back of it, 'Accepted by Bingley, set for and thrown out of the *North Briton* 21 June, on account of the Lord Mayor's death'. He added a reckoning of what fees he had lost and what he had 'gained in Elegies' by Beckford's demise. He found himself in pocket by exactly £3 13s 6d.

At this time Chatterton was lodging with a cousin. The other lodgers seem to have liked him well enough even though he was as 'proud as Lucifer'. The poor boy lived at subsistence level on bread and water with an occasional tart or a sheep's tongue. Now he was writing to live. He turned out pot-boilers quite literally; odes and elegies, sketches and short stories flowed from his pen and even a little opera. This burlesque, called 'The Revenge', was successfully produced during his first year in London, 1770.*

As he became poorer, so he was less and less willing for his friends to see his grinding poverty. He left the security of his cousin's lodgings and went to Holborn to be out of sight and out of mind. It is heart-breaking to imagine this gifted boy's plight, refusing to let his relations and friends know his true situation, unable to find a patron to foster his genius and with a temperament that must have caused him to suffer quite excruciating distress of mind. Pitifully he sent off a parcel of china, with a snuffbox and two fans for his mother, sister and grandmother. Little can they have dreamt that these little gifts represented some of his last earnings, in a gesture of gallant prodigality. This last desperate attempt to hide his poverty from his relatives, this pride which he could not overcome, also prevented him from getting any job to help him survive. He would not humble himself. Up to the very last he talked to neighbours in the old didactic manner, discussing, as he used to do with his young schoolfellows, politics and art, philosophy and literature. After refusing even to accept invitations to meals, though he did on one occasion devour some oysters, this unhappy child of seventeen, who must have often contemplated suicide, was found one August morning by his landlady. He had not spared himself anything. He lay in the ghastly distortion brought about by having swallowed arsenic and water. What an appalling tragedy and waste. The floor of his room was littered with scraps of torn up paper, maybe a final poem. A few weeks before he killed himself he wrote his last 'Rowley' poem. He called it 'Ballade of Charitie'.

'THE CLEVER, LIVELY, CHARMING MOZART'†
1756–1791

One of the best known examples of this rare breed, the infant prodigy, was little Wolfgang Amadeus Mozart, known in his family by the pet-name of 'Woferl'. The excuse for including him

---

*See *Oxford Companion to English Literature* edited by Sir Paul Harvey. Another writer says it was paid for but never performed.
†Count Zinzerdorf's description.

amongst a practically exclusively English company of children and families is the successful appearances he made in England, as we shall see.

Wolfgang came from a comfortably off, middle-class, musical family who lived in the small cathedral town of Salzburg. His father was a composer and musician, so the child's genius was nourished on fertile soil. The boy wrote his first composition at the age of five, and his first public appearance was when he sang in a choir, also at the age of five. Though he was never renowned for his looks, he had blue eyes and a radiant personality. He must have inherited his mother's gay, cheerful character, for he seems to have been a happy child in what most of us would have considered very adverse conditions, when, at six years old, he and his sister Nannerl,* who was eleven, traipsed all over Europe, giving concerts with that outstanding showman, their father Leopold Mozart.

The children had always been kept busy practising music and learning languages and the three Rs, though Leopold kept the four year old Wolfgang's musical powers secret at first from all but a few of their close friends.

The concerts were immensely successful. The Emperor Franz I and Maria Theresa, patronised the concerts, but apparently were more astonished by the little boy's composed appearance as he played quite unselfconsciously and unabashed by his audience, than by his truly remarkable musical talents.

'My children', wrote Leopold in July 1763, 'have set all Schwetzingen talking. The Elector and his consort have shown indescribable pleasure and everyone has been amazed'. Wolfgang was then seven. The same year, in August, the father wrote from Frankfurt, 'Wolfgang is extraordinarily jolly, but a bit of a scamp as well'. This comes as rather a relief. The little prodigy was delightfully human, and his own letters to his family are gay and spontaneous: by the time he was thirteen they were laced with a hotch-potch of German, Italian and Latin. He was quite a linguist, and arithmetic came easily to him as well.

No letters exist to date describing the first tour in 1762; but Goethe, then himself only fourteen, went to one concert in 1763, when Wolfgang was seven, and he told a friend much later that he still remembered 'the little fellow with his wig and sword'. In those days children were dressed like miniature adults. One unusual feature of this gifted boy's concerts was that he did so much ex-

*Pet-name for Marianne.

24

temporising. His father, with Germanic thoroughness, saw to it that the boy's amusements, too, were connected with music.

Leopold frequently wrote in his letters about putting the children's health before everything, which was, of course, a laudable aim. We must be pardoned all the same for wondering if this was not said to calm the anxieties of Mrs Mozart. Wolfgang was often ill, and

Leopold Mozart with his two children, Wolfgang and Nannerl (Marianne), 1777. Picture by Carmontelle (Louis Carrogis). Courtesy of the Musée Carnavalet, Paris.

no wonder, with that restless and exacting life, living in bitterly cold, unheated lodgings, and always tired however good might be his spirits. Chills, toothache, colds and fever dogged the children and it rather looks as though at least some of the causes of Mozart's early death stemmed from his exhausting childhood.

Praise and appreciation followed them wherever they went, of course, but what an exhibitionist Leopold was, more especially in London when he showed off his infant prodigies as though they were a music-hall act. In fact, the London visit did not take place until Mozart was eight, when a notice advertised him as 'the greatest prodigy that Europe or that even Human Nature has to boast'. Leopold made the boy play on the keyboard with a cloth held over his hands and various tricks of a similar kind.

Leopold was certainly not slow-witted as a business man. He complained, with some reason, when Princess Amalie, sister of Frederick II of Prussia, made the children play to her at Aachen, but had no money with which to reward them. He wrote tartly, '. . . if the kisses that she gave to my children, and to Wolfgang especially, had been all new Louis d'or, we should be quite happy; but neither the innkeeper nor the postmaster are paid in kisses'.

However, the children were generally overwhelmed with gifts from their admirers, even if Leopold was rather scornful of these little tributes; the swords, the Dutch lace, the cloaks and snuff-boxes, the toothpicks, the *étuis* and 'such stuff'. In fact, remarked Leopold, 'we shall soon be able to rig out a stall', but he added, characteristically, that he hoped the concert at Brussels (November 1763) the next Monday, would 'haul in plenty of fat thalers and louis d'or' when Prince Karl of Lorraine was to be present.

The Mozarts were given the chance to appear at Versailles, thanks to the good offices of Baron Friedrich Melchior von Grimm, a German who lived in Paris. Young Wolfgang sensed at once that this suave, man-of-the-world was not to be trusted, and he formed an instant dislike to him which was, much later, to be fully justified. The antipathy appears to have been mutual, though he impressed Leopold by his gift of a gold watch to Nannerl and a fruit-knife set in gold and mother-of-pearl with two blades for Wolfgang. It was customary to use such a knife on glacé fruits in Paris. Leopold is protesting too much, with his exaggerated praise of this miserable fruit-knife, which does not compare very favourably with Nannerl's gold watch. However, now, in the late December of 1763, the Mozarts arrived triumphantly in Paris and were received at Versailles where Leopold admired the charms of Madame de Pompadour, 'extremely haughty and still rules over everything'. Four months later she was dead; she was only forty-three. Wolfgang received the usual charming presents, Madame la Comtesse de Tessé gave him a snuff-box and a gold watch, whilst the Princess Carignan offered him a miniature silver pocket writing-case, complete with silver pens, for him to use when writing his composition. Wolfgang was kissed by the royal ladies, a remarkable honour, and his father noted that genuflections and bows were not expected when the king passed by. 'One remains erect and immovable.' Wolfgang was also allowed to stand by the Queen (Maria Leczinska) at mealtimes, where he was handed dishes from the table by Her Majesty, who was able to speak German, though the King could not. 'My children' wrote Leopold complacently, 'have taken almost everyone by storm'. Tantalisingly he does not qualify the 'almost'. Could it have been Grimm, the friend of such remarkable men as Diderot and Rousseau, who was not amongst the majority of ecstatic admirers? This is unlikely, as their success would resound to the credit of their patron, who is eulogised by Leopold as 'a man of learning and a great friend of humanity'. No wonder he was so grateful to Grimm, as none of his other letters of recommendation helped them at all.

Life was very expensive at Versailles. They had to go about in sedan-chairs at 12 sous a drive, as no *fiacres* or *carosses de remise* were available. The Mozart family stayed at a small hotel called the *Cormier*, rue des Bons-Enfants, appropriately enough, and found, like everybody else, that French innkeepers charged enormous prices for very poor accommodation. In fact, they spent what was then the huge sum of 26 louis d'or in 16 days. Father and son made a point of attending mass in the Royal Chapel so as to hear the choir. The famous water-colour picture of Leopold playing a violin, Wolfgang, now eight, at the harpsichord, and Nannerl singing was painted in April, 1764 by Louis Carmontelle (1717–1806). It is now in the Musée Condé, Chantilly. The picture was engraved by Delaforze, thus enabling it to reach a larger public. Another very well-known painting is *Thé à l'Anglaise* by Michel Barthélémy Ollivier (1712–1784) which shows Wolfgang playing for the company at the Prince de Conti's house. Ollivier was patronised by the Conti family. As usual, gifts were showered on the young Mozarts, and they went away with numbers of priceless snuffboxes of crystal set in gold and *vernis martin*, inlaid with flowers of coloured golds, as well as rings, flowers, ribbons and many other tokens of admiration. Alas, sore throats, fevers and colds persisted in Paris, too, but on they went as soon as they had recovered. Their spirits were undaunted by illness, though this surely took a toll of their future health and stamina. Tickets for their Paris concerts had Leopold's seal on them and the words '*Au Théâtre de M. Félix, rue et Porte St Honoré, ce . . .* (date), *à six heures du soir*'. The tickets were sold by friends the week before the concert, as no payment was allowed at the door.

Leopold reported in a long letter dated Paris, 1–3 February 1764, that 'four sonatas of M. Wolfgang are being engraved. Picture to yourself the furore which they will make in the world when people read on the title page that they have been composed by a seven-year-old child'. 'The Oeuvre 1e of engraved sonatas' was dedicated to Madame Victorine, Louis XV's second daughter, and this was Mozart's first printed work.

Now came the visit to London, for 15 months; the departure from Paris being on 10 April. They certainly did not let the grass grow under their feet. Leopold wrote from London on 25 April, 'Thank God we have crossed the Maxglanerbach★ . . . we have not done so without making a heavy contribution in vomiting'. The most important event, musically, which happened to Wolfgang in London was his introduction to the circle of Johann Christian Bach and Karl Friedrich Abel, pupils of Johann Sebastian Bach†; the world, in fact, of the Italian Opera; for in the eighteenth century it was to Italy that musicians looked for the model on which to build.

Young Wolfgang once more fell a prey to illness, but whilst recovering from it he wrote a series of compositions called the 'London Sketchbook'. Moreover he was the subject of a learned naturalist-cum-lawyer's★★ tests, subsequently published in a scientific work, which attempted to analyse the source of the child prodigy's 'mystery'. Another landmark of the London trip was the development of the child, playing music as a game, into the child with his own particular talents, that he thought of now as work rather than play. In 1765, now nine years old, the brilliant composer produced his sonatas, Opus 3, for the young English Queen. Now he had passed from the bud to the flower and was producing his own work and not just playing the creations of other musicians. Leopold noted the easy manners and friendly ways of George III and Charlotte. They were, of course, young at this time, the King being 27 and his Queen only 21. They both loved music and Charlotte played and sang reasonably well. King George's favourite composer was Handel. The summer of 1764 was an unqualified success for Wolfgang, playing everything the King asked for '*prima vista*' as his proud father said. The King placed before the little prodigy works of Bach, Handel, Abel and Wagenseil, the Empress Maria-

---

★This was a family joke, the name they gave to the English Channel.

†Johann Christian was Bach's youngest son. He had 20 children.

★★Daines Barrington (1727–1800).

Theresa's music master. The boy played the organ and the clavier and sang with the Queen and then improvised some melodies on airs by Handel. 'He exceeds all that one can imagine', exclaimed the delighted father. Money, as well as praise, flowed in. They took one hundred guineas in three hours. The leading families of England, the ambassadors and royalty all flocked to hear the infant prodigy. Except for the unfortunate illness of poor Leopold, the London visit was very worth while indeed, in spite of the unwise step of presenting the gifted children as 'spectacles', which was not a success.

The enthusiasm for the prodigies, however, was beginning to wear thin and, what with illnesses that attacked each of the family in turn, the next tour to the Hague, via Lille, Ghent, Antwerp, Rotterdam and Amsterdam, was depressing for Leopold. The sick Wolfgang managed, nevertheless, to compose more and more incomparable music and, after two year's travel, they arrived at Paris again. Here too, according to Grimm, they were no longer a sensation; and although Wolfgang wrote a '*Messe à Paris*' their second visit was not a happy one. They went on to Switzerland, but although Voltaire wanted to hear 'le petit Mozar', Leopold refused to let his children perform to the sick, godless 'arch-rogue', who was himself very ill. A Swiss doctor of considerable eminence, called Tissot, studied the young ten year old composer and shrewdly commented that he would eventually be 'one of the greatest masters of his art'. So the peregrinations round Europe continued until, at long last, the weary little prodigies arrived back in Salzburg in November 1766. Nannerl was a young lady of sixteen and Wolfgang almost eleven. He spent a period of enforced idleness when smallpox attacked him, and his return to Vienna was not as enthusiastic and triumphant as they had all hoped, due to the people's fear of smallpox. The Emperor Joseph and Maria Theresa were encouraging, however, and the Emperor commissioned an Italian opera buffa from the 12-year-old composer. It was not performed in the spring of 1768, as expected, due to jealousies and intrigues, and now Leopold decided to go to Italy, the mecca for all eighteenth century musicians.

Perhaps, now, he could no longer be called the infant prodigy, and we will leave him on a note of hope and cheerfulness, preparing to visit Verona, Milan, Bologna, Florence, Rome and Naples, amongst other places. On 13 December 1769, still scarcely fourteen, he wrote from Worgl, en route for Italy, to his mother: 'Dearest Mama, My heart is completely enchanted with all these pleasures . . .'.

29

And how much pleasure this amazing child would be leaving for all of us to enjoy ever afterwards.

WILLIAM BETTY, THE YOUNG ROSCIUS
1791–1874

There is nothing particularly unusual about an acting prodigy. Many famous theatrical families have produced them. Edmund Kean (1787–1833) appeared as a 'pupil of nature' at a tender age. Maude Adams, born in 1872, played all the child roles in the San Francisco Theatre, including Eva in *Uncle Tom's Cabin*; Ira Frederick Aldridge (1804–1867), billed as 'the African Roscius' went on to be enormously successful in his day and toured all over Europe. The Terry family saw Kate playing Prince Arthur in Charles Kean's production of *King John* at eight years old and Ellen Terry appeared in *The Winter's Tale* at the age of nine. The list is long and illustrious of children with natural ability born into a stage family automatically treading the boards from their earliest years. Just the same happened to Circus families. The famous Joseph Grimaldi (1778–1837) was the son of Guiseppi Grimaldi, ballet-master at Drury Lane. Joe danced at Sadler's Wells at the age of two years and three months and whilst only a boy he played the parts of dwarfs and old hags. The famous Rachel (1820–1858) appeared in many different parts between the ages of thirteen and sixteen. A prodigy called Jean Davenport appeared in a huge range of characters from 1837. She took the parts of Richard III, Shylock, and the Young Norval, as well as Sir Peter Teazle. She is supposed to be the original of Dicken's immortal Ninetta Crummles. Leigh Hunt wrote out what he called 'An Accurate List of Infant Prodigies' which comprised:

> The Infant Billington
> The Infant Columbine
> The Young Roscius
> The Younger Roscius
> The Young Orpheus
> The Infant Vestris
> The Comic Roscius.

These were all theatrical infants, and there were many more besides.

However, the Young Roscius was the only one who was not born into the profession but set the whole of London alight with what Byron called 'Rosciomania', a word he coined in 1804 to describe the fever of excitement the beautiful young Irish boy roused in fashionable society. He came flushed with success after a triumphant and presumably utterly exhausting tour of Ireland, Scotland and the Provinces.

The boy's career was as fleeting as it was sensational. He was born at Hopton Court in Shrewsbury, 'an extensive manor' inherited by his poor, timorous, brow-beaten mother. This shadowy figure only appears in the wings as she tries to snatch a few hours of natural childhood for her unfortunate prodigy with his own age-group. He was doomed to spend nearly all his time with adults.

His father was the eldest son of an Irish physician who left him with an estate and a fortune. That was no good to Mr Betty. He was like Parson Woodforde's 30-year-old curate friend Castres Donne, who wrote in a letter that 'gold will never find in my Breeches an abiding City'. Mr Betty was an even greater tyrant than Mozart's father, and even more avaricious for money. He was a real adept at spending money and when he discovered his son's talent for acting was negotiable, he decided to turn the boy's astounding good looks and acting ability into hard cash. There is reason to believe★ that the male side of the ecstatic audiences which thronged to watch our infant prodigy was particularly susceptible to his admittedly feminine style of charms. It seems at least possible that the dismissal, so disastrous as it turned out to be, of the 'theatric tutor' Hough may have been caused by this magnetic appeal. The odd circumstances of his departure were never satisfactorily explained and in the long future of his life off the stage William Betty never would discuss Hough nor was his name included in a biography written by an anonymous author who had presumably learnt his facts from the disappointed middle-aged actor in 1846. Only after Master Betty's death in 1874 did the forgotten name of his tutor Hough crop up again. As Mr Giles Playfair points out in his fascinating biography *The Prodigy*, though the pointers towards Hough's perverted tendencies are there we have no proof, only conjecture. The boy was undoubtedly extremely handsome and he must have had considerable talent, if only to be able to follow his tutor's instructions to the letter. He was said to be an exceptionally receptive pupil. It does not look as if he was able to act without the support of an instructor as we shall see later. Perhaps this unlucky boy's tragedy was that his gold-greedy father and the ambitious tutor Hough, called by his contemporaries his 'Friends', exploited his gifts, building up the hope of lasting genius which was beyond the boy's capacity to fulfil.

★*The Prodigy* by Giles Playfair, 1967.

He was wildly acclaimed on his first appearances in Belfast as a 'phenomenon of the age'. There was, as we have seen, quite a few of these about at the time. Master Betty was hailed as the 'minor Roscius' in Belfast and graduated to the 'Infant Roscius' in Dublin,

William Betty, known as the 'Young Roscius'. Courtesy of the National Portrait Gallery.

till in Cork he became the 'Young Roscius' for all time. Mr Betty and his stage-manager William Hough were past-masters at the art of puffing as it was called in those days. Rosciomania had begun in earnest and the playbills, advertising favourable comments from the newspapers, surpassed themselves. They described audiences drenched in tears, astonished and lost in wonder. Hollywood had nothing on Georgian England, the Scottish and the Irish press.

This was, of course, an age of enthusiasm and hyperbole when it was fashionable to talk in exaggerated language. For instance, nobody was in the least surprised when John Jackson, an ex-actor, who owned Glasgow and Edinburgh theatres, engaged Master Betty and described him as 'presented by Heaven and fully instructed by the inspiring voice of nature'. We have always as a nation been suckers for the brilliant amateur. It is so much more attractive than the tortoise-like dogged-does-it type. To call the boy a natural genius would have been too flat and moreover it would not have 'sold' the boy so well to his audiences. Master Betty was clearly extremely well drilled in his training but his public preferred the image of the Boy Wonder, the reincarnation of their never-to-be-forgotten lost Garrick, now miraculously restored to them in the shape of this 'glorious, incomparable, inimitable boy'. They just did not like understatement.

Poor little William Betty, who had been taken to see Mrs Siddons in Belfast when he was nearly eleven in the summer of 1802, is quoted as saying, 'I shall certainly die if I may not be a player'. This remark was a godsend to his father who made use of it to demonstrate that the boy had always been determined to act. The miracle was that he lasted as long as he did under the superlatives of salesmanship that turned him from a very good-looking boy, rather young for his age, gifted with some talent and much personal magnetism, into the darling of the fashionable world.

One great mistake that the tutor and the father both made was to boast about their prodigy's success, lauding him as better than Mrs Siddons. They pointed out that she had been unable to draw people for seven nights whereas the Young Roscius had performed fourteen times in Glasgow to huge audiences. The adult actors and actresses were not amused to observe that the 11-year-old prodigy was able to command high prices too, garnering 50 to 100 guineas a night even before he reached London. It's never a good idea to make enemies in your chosen profession.

His father's greed for money at the expense of the boy's health and carefree childhood is quite appalling. The gentle, easily intimidated mother seems to have been unable to do a thing about it. In

33

spite of Hough's mealy-mouthed assurances that Young Roscius must not play oftener than three nights in a week, the boy was compelled to present thirteen performances in Birmingham in thirty days and less than three weeks later he appeared fourteen times in nineteen days, of which the last six performances were consecutive. The unfortunate prodigy must have been utterly exhausted and indeed we are told that 'strengthening pills' and rum and milk were constantly administered. He was forced by his unfeeling father and tutor to go without sleep in order to give extra performances during these hectic tours round the provinces prior to his London début. Nor did his day end when the performance of the play was finished. The whole Royal Family came under his spell after his arrival in London and we hear that the future Lady Caroline Lamb was 'raving wild with Master Betty', so that social invitations became part of the boy's duties. Nevertheless he was not entirely starved of amusements with young company. On Sunday 13 April 1805 when he was at last in London he went to stay with the Marquis of Abercorn at Bentley Priory, Stanmore. He went in company with both his parents and we are told, ' . . . He has received many valuable presents, particularly from the Marquis, who is immoderately fond of him . . . The Marquis and his sons . . . breakfasted together very early. About 2 o'clock Lord Claude Hamilton and the Young Roscius were in the habit last week of amusing themselves on the serpentine lake in the gardens with rowing . . . or in fishing for carp . . .'. A few days later he was visiting the circus at Astley's.

One of the few voices raised to press for the Wonder Boy's protection described how he was carried out 'as a log of wood with hardly any sensation' after playing five nights running in 'deep tragedies'. The whole picture is quite Dickensian as we listen to the terrible Mr Betty and the grasping tutor Hough explaining that the boy yielded to public demand in giving extra performances, 'out of his own generosity of spirit'. We cannot believe it. If he was not too drained of vitality to appreciate it, then possibly the ringing of church bells in honour of his agreeing to extra performances may have pleased him; but what of the supporting actors? They must have found it exhausting too, with very little honour and glory to compensate them; though let us hope they were given extra cash. Master Betty was netting for his 'Friends' £1,500 for 15 performances in the provinces.

Now he was daringly advertised as a second Garrick. Bettymania could go no further, they may have thought. But London was still to come. Present day audiences may remember how easily we in our turn fell victims to the publicity puffs for Rudolf Valentino, Greta Garbo, Marilyn Monro, the Beatles and their followers with much the same hysteria which was engendered by publicity agents rather than by spontaneous combustion.

There is something not only ludicrous but also nauseating about the scramble to procure Master Betty for the London stage. Drury Lane and Covent Garden bid against each other to engage a child to take the best parts from their finest actors. The answer to the undignified competition was of course money, and quick money at that. Sheridan was just as eager to lay hold of the little goose that produced the golden eggs as his rival Thomas Harris of Covent Garden. Sheridan probably remembered with some exasperation how he had ignored Mr Hough's letter in 1803 asking for his 'protection' of Master Betty.

The Wonderful Boy appeared first at Covent Garden on 1 December 1804 in a tragedy long since forgotten called *Barbarossa*. His first appearance at Drury Lane was to be on 10 December. What a swooning and clapping and buzzing of excited conversation there was before the play and afterwards 'a thundering crack of applause such as I thought I never heard before', reported the diarist and painter Joseph Farington. Another artist, James Northcote wrote, 'He and Buonaparte now divide the world'. The press was equally enthusiastic and the Duchess of Devonshire wrote to her son, '. . . nothing is hardly seen or talked of but this Young Roscius . . . He is but 13 and yet I never saw anything to compare to him'. Lady Bessborough wrote on 5 December 'Nothing is heard from morn to night but praise of poor little Betty who will be kill'd with it, for they make him act every night'.

She was right, for on 18 December Mr Betty wrote to Sheridan's manager announcing that his unfortunate little goose had collapsed and was under the care of two doctors. On Christmas Day he was still extremely weak and ill and in fact he did not go back to work until the end of January (1805). You may be sure that his 'Friends' saw to it that he began again the instant his doctors pronounced him fit.

For his short period of convalescence he had been invited to Bushey Park, in company with his shadowy mother and ambitious father, by the Duke of Clarence, who had already given a supper party in his honour in St James's Palace before Christmas. What sort of a rest that was can well be imagined. The newspapers were more considerate than his parents and promoters over the combination of extremely hard work acting every night, followed by exhausting parties. The *Daily Advertiser* remarked that it was 'no

35

doubt highly gratifying for his friends that he should be noticed by His Grace (the Duke of Clarence), but to sit up till two or three in the morning, eat all sort of mixtures and drink all sort of wines' was far from the best cure for the 'violent fever' he had been suffering from since at least 2 December (1804). The *Morning Post* had then protested at the exploitation of Master Betty. 'Is it not a crime to make a child of 13 . . . act every night in a large theatre, the most arduous parts of the tragedies represented?' His poor mother, in her ineffectual way, always tried to counterbalance the long hours of hard work in favour of play, but Mr Betty was every bit as eager as Mr Mozart had been in showing off his prodigy and gleaning as much hard cash as possible from his talents. Perhaps it was not quite so strange in those days of using children in the mines, in the factories and as chimney-sweeps, but today such unscrupulous battening on child labour is utterly distasteful, more especially in a parent.

Svengali, in the shape of the tutor William Hough, was eventually dismissed in the Spring of 1805. Whether he *was* a Svengali or whether he had to go because, as we have seen, the Young Roscius may have had a 'fatal attraction' for him, can only be guessed. There is a discreet veil drawn over the true reason for his departure. Certain it is that from the moment that Hough left the already discernible signals of decline from popular darling of the fashionable world had set in. Even Mr Betty, insensitive as he was, saw the writing on the wall. In December, 1805, the press was in full cry against Mr Betty if not yet against his unfortunate son. All the various means Mr Betty was using to acquire extra money from his Wonderful Boy were pin-pointed. There was the attempt to prevent Opie and Northcote from showing their pictures of Master Betty at the Royal Academy lest sales of the prints were affected, for which Mr Betty held the rights; the benefit performances in aid of various charities were also refused. Then came the return of Kemble in the part of Othello at his own theatre and although Mr Betty had signed on both at Drury Lane and Covent Garden for a second London season in December, it was now clear that even though Master Betty was still welcomed uproariously in the provinces, the boy's attractions in fickle London society were beginning to fade. Fashions change indeed as easily as the wind and when, amongst a positive rash of infant prodigies, who of course had jumped on the Young Roscius's bandwaggon, a young Miss Mudie was treacherously produced by Kemble himself knowing her limitations, her performance was a disastrous occasion that threw discredit on the whole race of prodigies.

Leigh Hunt, still only twenty-one, sounded the Young Roscius's death knell writing as dramatic critic for his brother's weekly paper *The News*: '... We are surprised neither at money-getting managers nor at money-getting fathers; if the people will be deluded, they may as well be deluded with *astonishing infants* as with *astonishing horses* and *astonishing five-legged rams* ... But we shall be surprised if the delusion lasts; the introduction of children on the stage in characters irreconcilable to their age and size is systematically absurd ...' So strong had been the magic up till now that hardly a voice had been raised to make this obvious point. Bettymania was deflated at last. Could Leigh Hunt have been put up to this by Kemble? Mr Betty began to scent danger for his goose. The voices of the enemies' campaign grew louder and louder. Leigh Hunt debunked the boy as he had already flattened Miss Mudie. Mr Betty hung on, his assets in 1806 were about 50 per cent down on the benefits of the previous year and his son appeared less often, nor was he engaged for a third London season. He did continue to act in the provinces where his remembered image conjured up enthusiastic audiences, but he was fifteen now and his voice was breaking. This was the final blow.

What happened to cause the fall of the idol? A combination of events? The dismissal of Hough, the enmity of the adult actors, the capricious public requiring new titillations of its senses? Or was it simply that the reverse process of caterpillar into butterfly took place when the beautiful child with a golden voice became the lumpy adolescent with a broken voice? His public could not reconcile themselves to the prodigy who had matured into an ordinary, not very talented actor. Childhood beauty can change into ungainly shapes and Master Betty's acting talent may have been little more than obedient mimicry of a brilliant tutor's instruction. The Young Roscius may have had little personality of his own and possibly not much brains to tide him over the hurdle of unattractive adolescence.

At last the father saw that he must give up the struggle and try to educate his son for an ordinary man's place in the world. In the summer of 1808 Master Betty, now seventeen, was entered as a commoner of Christ's College, Cambridge. He called himself William Henry West-Betty. He had been appearing from time to time in small provincial theatres since the end of his London triumphs, but his father could not squeeze any more money out of a has-been prodigy, even though he must have still had a certain talent, if Macready is to be believed.

At twenty Master Betty made an effort to return to the London stage via the provincial circuit as he had done in the early years. His appearance at Covent Garden was received quite well by the audience but with venom by the critics. 'The world will never admire twice', remarked Northcote.

At the height of his fame there were all too many fortune-hunters ready to cash in on the side-lines inspired by the theatrical prodigy. Besides Mr Betty with his ever empty pockets to be filled and the needs of the tutor Hough, who certainly did not jump on the 'Friends' bandwaggon for nothing, there were other purses waiting to be filled by the hero-worshipping public. Everyone was aching to buy engravings of Master Betty, statuettes, marble busts, medals which had been struck with his likeness to advertise his London début and even head-dresses and fashionable clothes inspired by the Young Roscius's performances. Poems were written in his honour; and those enterprising publishers of children's books, Messrs S. and J. Fuller of The Temple of Fancy, Rathbone Place put 'Young Albert the Roscius' into their delightful series of paper-doll books. The Birmingham Museum has a copy of the third edition of this charming publication, which is dated 1811, when poor Master Betty's career had ended. He was then twenty and forgotten in London though he still toured the less fickle provinces. The book is, however, prophetic:

'Enamour'd now of SHAKESPEARE'S page,
Ambition prompts to tread the stage;
of ROSCIUS now he feels the inspiring flame;
He gets the tragedy by heart,
Enters the spirit of each part,
And struts, a little candidate for fame'.

Assuredly he got his fame. He is one of the best known of infant prodigies and remembered by everyone interested in the theatre. He even rates an entry in the *Dictionary of National Biography*. His caricatures, busts, pictures, enamel boxes with his portrait on them and medals are all collected today.

Does his gentle ghost haunt Drury Lane and Covent Garden perhaps? Those long years of oblivion from the age of thirty-two, when he finally gave up the stage, to his death aged eighty-three in 1874 must have been hard to bear behind the mask he showed to his friends. They saw the ungainly figure, so disobligingly described by the handsome Byron in 1812. 'His acting is I fear utterly inadequate to the London engagement . . . His figure is fat, his voice unmanageable, his action ungraceful and, as Diggory★ says, "I defy him to extort that d——d muffin face of his into madness".'

★A character in a contemporary farce.

Poor bewildered Betty! It is pleasant to remember that in his hey-day the First Gentleman showed him over Carlton House and told Lady Elizabeth Foster afterwards that 'his manner was perfect; it was simple, graceful and unaffected'. Let us leave it at that.

WILLIAM ROWAN HAMILTON
A Mathematical Prodigy who Made Good
1805–1865

As we have already noticed very few infant prodigies in the field of mathematics seem to develop in later life into high ranking scholars. One who did was a boy called William Rowan Hamilton who was born in Dublic in 1805. His father was Irish and his mother of Scottish descent and they had a family of ten children, originally composed of six boys and four girls. His eldest brother died before he was born, and two younger children also died in infancy. 'Dear little Willy' was sent away when he was only just a year old to live with an uncle and aunt as his father and mother considered that he was sufficiently outstanding in development to be worth educating under the devoted care of the Reverend James Hamilton, a protestant curate at Trim in County Meath. This charming-looking county town with its ruined military castle and the river Boyne meandering peacefully through its fields was a pleasant environment for genius to flower in.

Uncle James had two sons and seven daughters, not to mention four children who died early. The Hamilton family certainly had their quivers full. In 1800 Uncle James had brought the 'Latin School', a charming Gothic-windowed house, the remains of 'Talbot's Castle', where not only Willy Hamilton eventually studied but also, much earlier of course, the young Arthur Wellesley, later Duke of Wellington. His family home, Dangan Castle, was in the neighbourhood. The school house was right beside the Abbey and it escaped intact when Cromwell reduced both Abbey and Castle to ruins.

Willy's father was a solicitor in Dublin, but an unlucky one. In spite of remarkable ability and energy he seems to have been dogged by misfortune and died at only forty-two, his wife having departed this life in 1817, two years before her husband. It was therefore very fortunate for Willy that he had the stable background of Uncle James' household to call his home.

At three years old this remarkable child not only read English fluently but was also well advanced in elementary arithmetic. It is perhaps worth remembering here that John Evelyn's son is recorded

39

as being able to read English, Latin and French at two-and-a-half. This child died very young. By five years old Willy was reading Latin, Greek, and Hebrew and reciting with great gusto long passages from Dryden, Homer, Milton and other poets. Between the ages of nine and ten he was learning Persian, Arabic and Sanscrit, topped up with some Indian dialects, and not forgetting that he had already tackled Italian and French with the same ease at the age of eight. Next he started on translating Virgil and Homer, nor did he neglect English literature, the Bible and Geography, quite apart from Mathematics, which was subsequently his most brilliant subject.

Certainly it is something of a relief to find that this outstanding child was by no means a prig. His aunt wrote to his mother on his third birthday telling her about her son's pugnacious attitude toward the other boys if they teased him. She says, 'he is as impudent as ever . . . and sometimes makes boys three times his age fly before him'. Aunt Sydney went on to tell her sister-in-law that her husband often called in the three-year-old Willy to read the Bible 'principally to shame some boys who are double his age'. Whatever this may have done to wound the amour-propre of the older boys it seems to have left Willy unscathed; if that did not make him a prig, obviously nothing could. Were these the boys perhaps whom he made fly before him?

At this tender age of three he was not only a very apt scholar, reported his aunt, but he never seemed to be able to sit still for a moment, so that she threatened to tie his legs together when he came for his lessons. When he was still only three Willy was provided with *Dr Johnson's Dictionary* and his uncle's method of teaching was first to make him learn to spell all the words of one syllable in that gigantic tome and afterwards to go on to the two-syllable words. This mammoth task, which the boy seems to have taken to like a duck to water, certainly ensured that he had a vocabulary not only far in advance of any child of his age, but also beyond a considerable number of adults as well.

Luckily for the child's balanced development he was also passionately interested in games. He told his aunt to report to his parents that he had grown into 'a famous leaper'. He also enjoyed digging in the garden and 'holding converse with imaginary wild beasts'. Aunt Sydney wrote that he had 'a great deal of roguery in him', thank goodness, even if he did ask his father to give him 'a nice little *globe* for a Christmas-box, the skeleton maps are too trifling *for his mind.*' Did he therefore inherit a sense of humour from his father who was a convivial man, 'much given to quizzing' and delighting in repartee, both fashionable attributes in Regency days? He certainly sounds from his aunt's letters a lively, active, playful and imaginative child. He also appears to have been gifted with tact. Once, at the age of five, when, by the way, he was already considered 'a good geographer' on top of all his other talents, Willy went out in a boat with companions gifted with much less exalted brains. He noticed that 'he was rather too high for his company' as Aunt Sydney put it, and adapted himself immediately by laughing and joking and talking nonsense. Such diplomacy in one so young is rare indeed. Willy Hamilton and Marjory Fleming were born within two years of each other, Marjory being his elder by two years. How amusing if they had met. Would they have liked each other? History is full of such unprofitable speculations.

By the age of five-and-a-half Willy was showing more signs of his mathematical genius. His uncle admitted that it was difficult to puzzle him in addition or multiplication. At eleven he compiled a Syriac grammar. At thirteen, now at school, he read Clairault's*
Algebra in French and composed an *Epitome of Algebra* which he entitled a *Compendious Treatise of Algebra by William Hamilton*. At the same date, about 1818, he wrote another grammar, this time of the Sanscrit language and also an *Analysis of a passage in Syriac*.

What is so unusual, when we consider the average child's laborious struggles to acquire knowledge, is that the infant prodigy regards his work as a game, a pleasure to enjoy. Willy had the infallible memory of a good scholar, as well as the scholar's delight in learning for its own sake for amusement rather than as a task.

He found a fellow-intellect in a talented American boy called Zerah Colburn when he was fourteen. Did Colburn become an average citizen in later life? Apparently 'his destination was the stage' wrote Willy to his sister, adding, 'Oh, what a fall was there!' This boy then excelled in mental arithmetic and his immensely long operations stimulated Willy to try to cultivate the same proficiency. In consequence he could for the rest of his life calculate square and cube roots by these speedy mental gymnastics. His letters at this time are also full of astronomical observations. At fifteen he began to study Newton's *Life* and *Principia*, but in his journal Willy is boy enough to crow happily about how he vaulted over two tables and three forms easily. He was also by now an expert swimmer. Nor does he lack interest in everyday events, following poor Queen Caroline's trial and noting down his opinions about her.

*A leading French mathematician.

At the age of eighteen our young genius was admitted to the membership of that august body the *Académie des Sciences* in Paris, having already presented a paper on geometry before them when he was only thirteen. What originally brought him to the attention of the learned world was that when he read the famous French scholar Laplace's book called *Mécanique Céleste*, he found an error in the great man's calculations. He wrote about his discovery to the Astronomer Royal of Ireland enclosing his suggested corrections. At seventeen, therefore, he was not only considered to be his native country's greatest scholar, but also he was acclaimed internationally. At the age of twenty-two he was appointed Professor of Astronomy in Dublin. In 1835, when he was only thirty, he was knighted.

If ever an infant prodigy made good, Willy Hamilton was one of that happy band. He spent the rest of his comparatively short life, for he died at the age of sixty, studying mathematics, astronomy and physics at Dublin University. He is chiefly remembered for his work on quarternions which 'may be called an algebra of vectors', to quote David Eugene Smith in *Scripta Mathematica* published in 1938.

It is difficult for us ordinary mortals, who have probably most of us never met an infant prodigy, to understand some of the problems of being blessed with such a splendid cuckoo in the nest. Nowadays the tendency in education seems to be to foster the less intelligent at the expense of the brilliant children.

I wonder what would have happened to Willy Hamilton if he had not had the advantages of his uncle's wise care in the pretty countryside of Trim. His father's influence and that of his Aunt Sydney, who alas died when he was nine, must also have helped him enormously.

Although many people are of the opinion that genius will inevitably make good, it is at least possible that in a different environment this very remarkable brain might have been lost to the world for want of proper nourishment and direction.

CHAPTER THREE

Children at Play

Toys to play with might be thought of as the first essential in a child's world, but as Mr Patrick Murray, Curator of the fascinating Museum of Childhood in Edinburgh, has pointed out*, life in the past was pretty grim for children. Except for imitating adults and kicking about stones and knucklebones of sheep, they must have been struggling for their very existence. Only comparatively recently, somewhere about 1700, can we begin the history of toys; though games and self-made entertainments would have been pretty well a matter of relying upon fertile imaginations. There, of course, lies the strength of a child. He can make a toy out of anything he can lay his hands upon. Look at the slumland toys in Mr Murray's museum, for instance. The doll made from an old shoe has more life and character in it than many a plastic beauty with a wardrobe of machine-made clothes, such as we buy for our daughters today. As for games, even the age-old ball, whether a football or a set of marbles, is only a means to an end. Any round stone would do. It is the adults who like more sophisticated toys, and it is inevitable that children will then accept and enjoy them. Whether they really like them better than the old shoe-doll is debatable. That one-eyed teddy-bear with an arm torn off by an angry friend is cherished far more than the new one Grandmother produced as a replacement.

Besides what we consider are the necessary toys and games, the more exciting visits *en famille* to places of amusement are always popular. Looking back into the past, we see that the children were provided with considerable attractions even before this age of press-button entertainment; so shall we take a look at some of the family amusements of long ago and see whether the eighteenth and nine-teenth century child was really much the worse off in that respect?

I

CIRCUSES, MENAGERIES, THEATRES AND FAIRS

A delightful picture belonging to the Marquess of Bath shows a late seventeenth century family, probably painted by Hans Eworth,

Toys by Patrick Murray.

'Seaside Frolics' by James Elder Christie, dated 1877. Courtesy of Sotheby's.

finishing a meal at a long table, covered by a white cloth. Besides the two parents, there are six children, one holding a pet marmoset, another with a goldfinch perched on his wrist, a third playing with a puppy trying to jump on to his lap. A green parrot is strutting amongst the fruit and wine on the table. Keeping private menageries dates back very far into history. In about 1680 B.C.* the Egyptians had a zoo full of monkeys, and in England Henry I collected deer, lions, a cheetah and a camel, as well as birds, and finally this menagerie, established first at Woodstock, Oxfordshire, was moved to the Tower of London by Henry III, though only in 1828 was it made into the famous zoo which we all visit today in Regent's Park.

In 1791 a certain Mr Burt compiled a useful guide for parents and sightseers to the menagerie, which was situated near the Strand in London. It was one of the earliest collections open to the general public and they were first allowed to see it in the early eighteenth

*Oxford Junior Encyclopaedia, 1950.

A large painted wooden rocking horse, 4 ft 2 ins high, on yoke rockers, *c* 1880–90. A familiar nursery toy. Courtesy of Sotheby's.

This pet cat masquerades as a night-light. The candle shows through the emerald green eyes. Late nineteenth century. Photograph by Jennifer May.

century. Mr Burt drew a few sketches, by way of advertisement, in order to demonstrate 'the Wonderful Works of the Omnipotent'. It must be confessed that some of the exhibits were purely sensational. A zebra, a heifer with two heads and an unfortunate negro, who unaccountably found his way into the collection, all figured in the enterprising Mr Burt's sketches of his attractions. There was a secretary bird, which had the reputation of being a very fine dancer. Another bird of this unusual variety was unlucky. It was on show at the Tower of London menagerie and pushed its foolish head inquisitively into a neighbouring cage. The hyena instantly bit off the secretary bird's head. Unluckily, foreign potentates made a habit of donating wild animals to the Tower of London menagerie. An early nineteenth century print shows children and their parents watching the antics of a bear on a pole, inside what looks an extremely inadequately fenced enclosure. At this time of the inauguration of the London Zoo, visitors were inclined to poke the exhibits with their parasols, or offer them remarkably unsuitable sustenance. In the early nineteenth century, the Royal Surrey Zoo was a particularly attractive one, with an arboretum encircling it with ponds and flower-beds, cages and aviaries, and many unusual exhibits such as the Andean condor, vicuna, leopard, lions, monkeys and parrots. By the 1850s this zoo attracted large crowds of families, not so much to see 'the timid and vivacious ocelot' as to witness splendid firework displays and visit the 'colossal Concert Hall' as well as the 'Fairy Caves'. By then, as it happened, the only animals advertised were a giraffe and a polar bear.

Queen Victoria herself visited the London Zoo in 1900 and sat on a stone which was patriotically retained as a memorial of the solemn occasion, and a beech tree was planted near it. Soon after, a giant tortoise was added to the group, to give weight perhaps to these tributes to Her Majesty's gracious patronage. The huge tortoise was believed to have been 160 years old. Although the Queen was only 4 feet 10 inches high herself, plump and very old, could there have been a subconscious connection in the minds of the zoo authorities between the ancient tortoise and the ancient Queen? Three giraffes arrived from the Sudan to delight the populace. These spectacular animals walked from the docks to the zoo, to the excited cheers of young and old alike. Apparently no awkward incidents occurred, apart from a demonstration from a mooing cow who caught sight of the new arrivals over a hedge in Commercial Road.

Travelling menageries were often combined with circuses or fairs, and mediaeval street-entertainers would appear with animals like monkeys and bears. These were familiar sights to children in the nineteenth century.

Life must have been full of excitement for children, even for the poorer ones. The rich could give parties and play amusing games like hide-and-seek all over the house. Remember the icy chiller by Henry James called *The Turn of The Screw*, when the children played this agonisingly enjoyable game with their highly sensitive new governess, who had pitted her strength against the powers of darkness, the evil spirit of the valet. In one ultra-religious household a party had to be preceded by prayers for guidance as to whether the small boy should be allowed to accept an invitation or not. Luckily God came down on the side of parties, on one occasion, but the father never gave Him another chance to guide his son in that reprehensible way again. Most children must have been to the fair and the circus, and even if such pleasures only came once a year, there was always the hope that the man with the 'raree show' might turn up. In a mid-Victorian oil painting of a family watching just such a man with his peep-show, there is a small, roughly made theatre, rather like a Punch-and-Judy show, on the top of a large box. The little theatre is showing 'Jack the Giant-Killer'; the man plays his pan-pipes and points with a thin wand to the special features of his show. The heavy box has 10 or 12 round holes with with small lids covering each hole. Two of the children have lifted the lids to see the exciting pictures inside. If only we knew what they were! It looks as if this raree show has been given a performance in a cellar and now only a few of the audience are left.

The toy theatre of the beginning of the nineteenth century made use of theatrical sheets of characters from current plays which were sold at stationer's shops. Scenery was soon added, always carefully accurate, and each play was made up of 10 or 20 sheets coloured in gay, vivid blues, greens, yellows and reds. They were twopence coloured and a penny for plain sheets. The first publisher, William West, had intended his sheets for an adult market, but very quickly children had taken them over for toys.

From about 1815 until 1835, juvenile drama flourished. About 50 publishers competed with William West in the business and jumped on his band-wagon. Immediately a new play was put on, it appeared in the toy theatre. It occupied pleasurably hundreds of nurseries and homes. The style of production went on till the 1850s, but deteriorated in engraving and colouring. By the second half of the nineteenth century, toy theatre sheets were give-away advertisements in magazines for children. Their interest lies in the vivid reproduction of the theatre and actors of the times with all the old

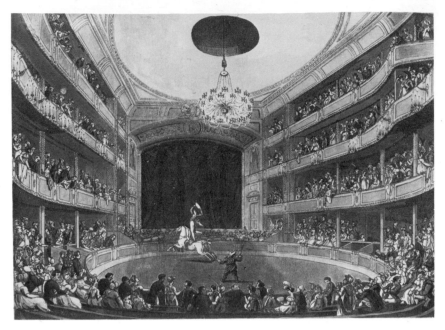

Astley's circus in full swing. Courtesy of the London Museum.

heroic gestures and even recognisable portraits of contemporary actors like Kemble, Vestris, Grimaldi and Kean. There are collections to be seen both at the British Museum and the London Museum. Interest has never quite expired, and sheets can still be bought in London at the famous Pollock's Toy Shop and Museum.

Toy theatres in countries such as Spain, Denmark and Germany grew up rather later, printed in colour lithography, but their plays were specially written for children and were 'not adapted from the living theatre'.

Puppets are so popular today, in their miniature theatres, that we must add them to this chapter. Their origin is ancient and world wide; probably they began in connection with religious ceremonies. Even today, in the Eastern countries, Buddhist traditional myths are still told by puppet showmen. Itinerant puppeteers in England were still performing biblical plays in the late eighteenth century, and every country in Europe took the family to travelling puppet theatres, whose plays generally brought to life legends and folk stories hundreds of years old. The puppeteers went to country fairs and villages, and were eagerly awaited by the children and their elders whose opportunity to see plays was rare.

One aspect of traditional puppet shows must have been watched with delighted horror; this was the mysterious 'Dissecting Skeleton' and the 'Grand Turk', which are still to be seen in certain companies today. These are mechanical trick puppets whose construction is guarded jealously. The skeleton dances for a while and then all his bones float apart and take on a life of their own as they dance individually on the tiny stage. The Grand Turk's disintegration takes the same form, but each limb turns into a little figure on its own. These two appeared, some years ago, in Wiltshire in Jan and Ann Bussell's enchanting performances.

The appeal of these minute theatrical entertainments found royal patronage on many occasions. Charles II saw the Italian puppets in London several times, and Pepys reported that Covent Garden was 'a great resort of gallants' to see the puppets. The Prince of Wales (Prinny) enjoyed Lord Barrymore's Puppet Theatre in 1790. There are several different types of puppet, besides the marionettes which we have just reviewed, and which are manipulated by wires or strings from above. The toy theatre, with its flat figures sometimes moved on straight wire rods from behind the stage, could be termed puppets and, of course, there were the shadow figures.

Punch and Judy are, surely, the best loved of all puppets and these are, of course, manipulated by hand from below the stage. The version we used still to see in the streets and seaside resorts up to the second World War took its form round about 1800 with dog Toby, who had no part in the *commedia dell'arte* from whom our Punch, and France's Polichinelle, derive. Pepys went to see a Punch-and-Judy show at Moorfields in 1666 which, he said, 'pleases me mightily . . . and I like the more I see it'. England, in fact, so much liked Polichinello that we were soon calling him Punch and adopting him as our own. He appealed to all ages. Dog Toby used to end the performance by carrying round a little bag in his mouth to collect coins from the audience.

The children in the last couple of centuries, and earlier, used also to go in for acting themselves, and school drama, performed by schoolboys, is found in dramatic literature of most European countries. There was considerable activity in this enjoyable pastime, which kept so many people busy and out of mischief, in the first half of the sixteenth century; and there are records of Boy Players, acting in Latin and English, being very fashionable in Queen Elizabeth's and James I's reigns. Boys at Eton, Winchester, Westminster, Shrewsbury and St Paul's, to mention only a few of the many schools, gave mostly classical dramatic performances, as did undergraduates, though by the seventeenth century this activity waned. The Prince Consort, however, took his son, the Prince of Wales, to see one of the traditional plays still surviving at Westminster, and in 1800 the Prince Regent went to one, and so did his brother William IV, in 1834.

What is so remarkable in these days of instant entertainments available to us all, from radio and television as well as sports galore, is that in the past also there were so many enjoyable outlets for family amusements. The first English pantomime was produced in 1716 by John Rich, an actor-manager who was a first class mimic. His shows quickly became favourite outdoor entertainments, specially at such great fairs as Southwark Fair. The puppet shows had been immensely successful before pantomimes encroached on their preserves. Illuminations were a form of celebration much in evidence at any national day of rejoicing like Waterloo, for instance. In Edinburgh everybody took a whole holiday, including the children of course. Listen to Catherine Sinclair's description of the fun in *Holiday House*: 'Frank and Henry were allowed to nail a dozen little candlesticks upon each window in the house . . . Any house not showing candles risked getting a stone through their windows. Some houses displayed paintings of Britannia, Mars, the Duke of Wellington, or St George slaying a dragon breathing out fire and smoke from its nostrils. After the candles had all burnt out the fireworks were let off on Castle Hill'.

Fairs, jugglers, performing animals, puppet shows, acrobats, fire-eaters, circuses and balloon ascents, all added to the gaiety of children in the past.

Two more glimpses into nineteenth century children's entertainment must be allowed. The first took place on New Year's Eve 1849. The Lord Mayor gave a Ball for children at the Mansion House. Several hundreds attended aged between seven and fifteen. Dancing began at 10 pm, and at 11 pm Mr Love the polyphonist 'introduced a variety of striking ventriloquial effects'. Supper followed, and then more dancing, and at midnight the gas-lights dimmed, to signify the old year going out, and then they were suddenly turned on again, 'giving a very pleasant effect'. The Mayor and Mayoress now *sat down* and shook hands with all their young guests, after a good time had clearly been had by all.

Secondly, we hear of rather a surprising Gunpowder Plot celebration which took place in aid of the *Merchant Seamen's Orphan Asylum*. The grounds of the institution were used to give a firework display and all was illuminated in the style Vauxhall still used. A band was playing, of course, but the oddest part of the

50

jollifications was that, in the back premises, a gibbet had been erected. On it was suspended an effigy of the Pope, surrounded by barrels of tar, 'which at the proper time were consumed in a formidable blaze'. The exhibition was attended by a large concourse of people, who, of course, benefited the charity funds considerably. Let us hope, nevertheless, that no foreigners came to those 'back premises' to see this indignity offered to their Pope.* Fair enough it may be to burn Guy Fawkes, but it seems rather excessive to burn the Pope in 1851! Whether the orphans were allowed to do more than watch from afar, we are not told; but they probably would not have minded whose effigy was put on the bonfire.

PLEASURE GARDENS FOR THE WHOLE FAMILY

One day in June 1665, Samuel Pepys noted in his famous Diary, that he went 'to the Spring Garden at Fox-Hall† and there stayed pleasantly walking, and spending but sixpence, till nine at night.' He added that 'it was the hottest day I ever felt in my life'. By the time that George I came to the throne the Vauxhall Garden had become a popular summer leisure-time resort for Londoners. These pleasure gardens were in their hey-day during the eighteenth century and people from all walks of life assembled there to dance, play cards, consume delicious syllabubs and cheese cakes, and to drink tea and coffee or ale and wines. There were in fact pleasure gardens before Pepys's day. For instance, Mulberry Garden was situated where Buckingham Palace now stands and at Charing Cross there were the Spring Gardens. The advantage of these places was that all the family from grandparents to the youngest toddler could go and amuse themselves there in the open air. Originally, no payment was required, except for food. Pepys records another happy day out: 'A great deal of company and the weather and garden pleasant and it is very cheap and pleasant going thither . . . But to hear the nightingale and the birds and here fiddles and there a harp and here a Jew's harp, and here laughing and there fine people walking is mighty divertising.' Some gardens belonged to a Spa. There were Spas, for instance, at Islington from 1684 to 1840; at Sadler's Wells from 1683, and Bagnigge Wells opened in 1759. London Spa, St Chad's Well, and Pancras Wells all started in the late seventeenth century. The most expensive and fashionable gardens were at Vauxhall and much later, in 1742, at Ranelagh. Families of a less choosy and humbler category, the tradesman and

*This was the 'no-Popery' period, of course.
†Vauxhall, subsequently.

51

E

A family outing in St James's Park. An engraving after a painting
by George Morland, 1790. Photograph by Studio Wreford.

his family, the journeyman tailors, hairdressers, milliners and
servant maids, who might be shy of rubbing shoulders with the
aristocracy, could go to New Georgia on Hampstead Heath, which
offered such amusements as a maze, mechanical oddities like a
collapsible chair or a pillory for young men to put their heads in to
receive hilarious kisses administered as punishment by the ladies
of the party. There were fireworks too or at least illuminations. The
London 'cit' and his family could find something to suit everyone.
Places with such cheerful names as the Queen's Head and Arti-
choke, the Jew's Harp House or the Yorkshire Stingo provided respectively tea, cakes and cream, skittles and 'bumble-puppy' with
shady bowers, a tennis court and a trap-ball ground. Best value,
perhaps, was the first one mentioned, as they offered concerts,
vaudevilles, 'comic burlettas' and occasional balloon ascents,
as well as fireworks on gala nights.

Other not so fashionable gardens, which had entertainments for
less sophisticated tastes provided comic songs, pantomimes, a
menagerie of animals, some of which were tame enough for the
children to stroke, sword-dances and tight-rope performances.

Monsieur and Madame Brila arrived from Paris with their three-year-old son, who exhibited 'several curiosities of balancing'. In 1745 a young giant, of fifteen years, came to these gardens, the New Wells near the London Spa. He was 7 feet 4 inches high. A year later the 'Saxon Lady Giantess' made her appearance. She was a mere 7 feet high. Oddly, considering these manifold attractions, the Wells closed about 1752, and the theatre was taken by the Rev. John Wesley and was turned into a Methodist tabernacle.

In 1710 a girl of nine sang several operatic songs very successfully at Hampstead Wells, when the gay and fashionable mingled with not only the London 'cit' and his family, but less respectable characters who eventually took over and the gardens consequently declined in popularity and finally closed down. It was here, incidentally, that *Evelina*★ was badgered to death by the unwelcome attentions of the insufferable Mr Smith at one of the Hampstead Balls in the Long Room, when he 'begged the favour of hopping a dance' with her.

It must have been amusing for the children to watch infant prodigies performing, like the two we have already mentioned, and 'the two wonderful posture makers', when a man and a child aged nine were presented in the dancing-room at the Wells.

In the hight of its popularity the Islington Spa Gardens† were frequented by the daughters of George II, Amelia and Caroline, who came to drink the waters. Mr Pinchbeck cashed in on the success of these gardens by selling his fans mounted with a specially designed view of the gardens. A song written in the 1730s told of the 'scrapes and curtsies, nods, winks, smiles and frowns, Lords, milkmaids, duchesses and clowns' who all assembled at Islington. No doubt light-fingered thieves were much in evidence too. Patrons might breakfast for ninepence, drink afternoon tea for sixpence, or take coffee at eightpence, served with cake or bread and butter. Besides all its other attractions a farce, written in 1770, remarked on another advantage. 'Oh, the watering-places are the only places to get young women lovers and husbands!'

Naturally all these pleasure gardens vied with each other for the different tastes of their customers. Most places provided tea and coffee, negus, punch, red port, ale, cyder and Rhenish or white wine. If, however, you went to Sadler's Wells the famous ale was brewed from the Spa waters and went down very well with some carraway comfits, perhaps, or preserved angelica which was well-

★Heroine of Fanny Burney's novel of that name.

†Also rather confusingly called the New Tunbridge Gardens.

known to comfort the stomach. The theatre and variety stage here were the chief attractions and in the eighteenth century it was the resort of 'strolling damsels, half-pay officers, peripatetic tradesmen, tars, butchers and other musically inclined'. Here came the famous clown Joseph Grimaldi in 1781, appearing in his monkey disguise, and there were Harlequinades, tumbling and rope-dancing. Even pony races were literally staged in 1862. In 1826 a balloon ascended from the grounds. Nearly 60 years before in 1785 the first man to make a balloon ascent in England, Vincent Lunardi, secretary to the Neapolitan Ambassador, had to descend unexpectedly at the Adam and Eve Gardens, causing enormous excitement. When Samuel Phelps joined the Sadler's Wells management in 1844 the plays he put on were almost entirely by Shakespeare.

Amongst all the multitude of Londoners, high, low and middling whom you might see at the pleasure gardens, were the notorious highwaymen. Bagnigge Wells was patronised by these villainous heroes, and the fictional Macheath in Gay's *Beggar's Opera* frequented Marylebone Gardens. History relates that Dick Turpin once publicly kissed a reigning beauty in Marylebone Gardens. The indignant lady expostulated angrily, at which the highwayman replied, 'Be not alarmed, madam. You can now boast that you have been kissed by Dick Turpin. Good morning!' In the late 1750s Marylebone Gardens was providing a speciality of almond cheese-cakes and rich seed and plum-cakes made by the Manager's daughter, which was clearly a popular collation.

A late eighteenth century print called 'Summer Amusement' shows children and dogs gaily frolicking with their elders. Another contemporary picture by George Morland gives an idyllic picture of a family having tea under the trees, the baby on its mother's knee, the eldest son making the little dog beg for some cake, and the stout little girl petting the dog with one hand and trundling along her toy horse-on-wheels with the other. Grandmama and Grandpapa are there too, preoccupied with the food, and the young husband is offering his wife something to eat. The picture is called 'A Tea Garden', an authentic representation of a typical day out. Rather a less idyllic family party is shown in a print called 'The Bayswater Tea Gardens, 1796'. Here Grandpapa has removed his wig and coat and grandmama fans herself as she sips her tea, whilst little Master offers his sister tea from a saucer and their dog looks up hopefully for his share of the feast.*

---

*The engraving appears in Woodward's *Eccentric Excursions* published in 1796 by Allen & West.

Pancras Wells specialised in refreshments, providing hot loaves, syllabubs, and milk straight from the cow. Here dinners were served and 'neat wines, curious punch, Dorchester, Marlborough and Ringwood beers'. One cannot help wondering what was so curious about the punch.

St Pancras Adam and Eve Tea Gardens had cows too; and pretty arbours, flowers and shrubs, tea-drinking and games of trap-ball and bowls as well as dinners could be enjoyed here. Cows were kept at White Conduit House also, and they supplied hot loaves, tea, coffee and refreshments 'in the greatest perfection'. Here they played cricket in 1754 in an adjoining meadow, the proprietor producing the bats and balls. Oliver Goldsmith used to visit this entertaining place and later on George Cruickshank came and made a number of his caricature sketches of local characters. Bowls, dutch-pins and archery, balloon ascents, concerts and firework displays were still being advertised here in 1825. In 1830 admission was two shillings. Ladies and children came in at half price.

Fashionable Belsize Park and its gardens was a favourite place for the Prince and Princess of Wales in 1721. 'Nobility and Laity' were encouraged by such treats as athletic sports, deer hunting, gambling and races, with music every day. A boys' race was another feature; the winner received a guinea. Another running race between the 'Cobler's Boy and John Wise, the Mile-End Drover' was also a matter of six times round the Park, the winner to receive a handsome 20 guineas. The Park, Wilderness and Gardens were about a mile in circumference.

The most famous of the pleasure gardens of course were Ranelagh and Vauxhall. At Ranelagh there was the celebrated Rotunda, which was originally called the Amphitheatre, and was designed by William Jones. Its first opening was in 1742. Horace Walpole wrote, 'I have been breakfasting this morning at Ranelagh Garden: they have built an immense amphitheatre with balconies full of little ale-houses: it is in rivalry to Vauxhall. 'Nobody', he wrote later, 'goes anywhere else. My Lord Chesterfield . . . says he has ordered all his letters to be directed thither'. The only weak spot, as with all the other gardens, was the English weather. Dr Johnson, Goldsmith, Reynolds, the Royal Princes all went to Ranelagh. It looked not unlike the Albert Hall, or should one say the Albert Hall is a pale imitation? Perhaps the nearest parallel is the Reading Room at the British Museum, which is almost exactly the same size. For more than 160 years it maintained its position, mixed company and all, as a fashionable resort. The people of what Walpole called 'true ton' tended to arrive about 11 pm. The citizens came to stare at the

Royal Dukes or any other celebrity who might turn up. The concerts were obviously very good indeed. In June, 1764 little Wolfgang Mozart* at the age of eight gave a recital on the harpsichord and on the organ, playing several of his own compositions. The Grand Jubilee Masquerades, in the Venetian Taste, which took place in April 1749 must have been worth seeing. Let Horace Walpole tell us about it: 'The Masquerade . . . was by far the best understood and prettiest spectacle I ever saw . . . It began at 3 o'clock; at five, people of fashion began to go . . . the whole garden was filled with masks and spread with tents . . . In one quarter was a Maypole dressed with garlands and people dancing round it to a tabor and pipe and rustic music, all masked, as were all the various bands of music that were disposed in different parts of the garden; some like huntsmen, some like peasants and a troop (sic) of harlequins and scaramouches in the little open temple on the mount . . . All round the outside of the amphitheatre were shops filled with Dresden china, Japan, etc., and all the shopkeepers in masks. The amphitheatre was illuminated, and in the middle was a circular bower, composed of all kinds of firs in tubs from 20 to 30 feet high; under them orange trees, with small lamps in each orange, and below them all sorts of the finest auriculas in pots; and festoons of natural flowers hanging from tree to tree . . . There were booths for tea and wine, gaming tables and dancing and about 2000 persons.'

Each masquerade or regatta was more splendid than the last until, about 1775, Ranelagh was suddenly 'voted a bore with the fashionable circles'. Although it revived again about 1790 for another decade, it then declined finally and both house and Rotunda were demolished in 1805.

Who of us walking along the Cromwell Road, remembers that once this part of London was Cromwell's Gardens? Later it was called Florida Gardens, Brompton, and here in the 1760s anyone might go and drink coffee or tea in its 'agreeable arbours', listen to music and watch equestrian feats performed. In 1781 the Gardens belonged to a German horticulturist who grew flowers, strawberries and cherries there and built a great dining-hall in the centre. Balloon ascents attracted the people and fireworks and a bowling green. Here they had an innovation in ice-creams to tempt the fickle public. Sadly the owner eventually became bankrupt like so many other over-ambitious proprietors of the smaller pleasure-gardens. Competition was too fierce.

*See also Chapter on 'Prodigies'.

As we have already seen pleasure gardens each had some speciality of their own and Bermondsey Spa offered a gallery of Paintings. Keyse's 'pictorial reproductions' of a greengrocer's stall and a butcher's shop were on show and many other works of a rather spectacular true-to-life kind, including a painting of Vesuvius and a *trompe l'oeil* painting of a candle which seemed as though it really was alight. Respectability rather than fashion was the keynote here. It was Mr Keyse's successors who were unable to make his project pay and it closed down about 1804 or 1805. The Keyse paintings were sold by auction. Where are they now, I wonder.

The Folly was notoriously dissipated, situated opposite Somerset House. It consisted of a strong barge or houseboat, where ladies of the town assembled and gambling took place. It was shut down in 1720. Another haunt of the dissolute was the Temple of Flora, on the left-hand side of Westminster Bridge Road, walking towards the Obelisk. Light refreshments of orgeat, 'confectionary', lemonade and strawberries and cream were served. Apollo Gardens was the resort of pickpockets and cheats of various kinds, although the owner boasted of patronage by the nobility and gentry. A smartly dressed young woman of eighteen nearly killed a poor child of ten, from whom she stole her sash in 1792. This 'infamous resort' closed down in 1796.

Lastly comes Vauxhall, which is surely the best known of all the London pleasure gardens. Its first flowering was from 1661 till 1728, which is rather too early for the period we are discussing. It is worth noting, however, that Swift visited the gardens in 1711 with a Lady Kerry and Miss Pratt in order to 'hear the nightingales'. All the early references seem to spell the word 'Fox Hall'.

In 1728 the true founder of Vauxhall Gardens at the height of its splendour and success comes on the scene. He was called Jonathan Tyers and he altered and improved all the various facilities and then opened it with great *éclat* in 1732. Visitors flocked here by the thousand and what is more, good order seems to have prevailed so that it kept its good name. The season tickets were made of silver and designed by Hogarth, and it was regularly patronised by Frederick, Prince of Wales, until he died in 1751. Everybody had to go to Vauxhall to be in fashion and the 'cits' who could afford the rather higher entrance fee than those of the smaller gardens came too. Handel was Master of Music at one time. There were attractions like the Cascade, announced by a loud bell at 9 o'clock, which was a spectacular illumination.

Their speciality in the way of food and drink was arrack, the famous punch which overcame Jos Sedley in *Vanity Fair*; Vauxhall

57

nectar, 'a mixture of rum and syrup with an addition of benzoric acid or flowers of benjamin' and 'slices of almost invisible ham' with chickens of a diminutive size, no bigger than a sparrow, someone said in 1755. The thin-ness of the ham and the smallness of the birds continued throughout the years. A writer in 1762 was re-marking upon the fact that he could read his newspaper through the slices of ham and beef provided so expensively at Vauxhall and the complaints continued under Queen Victoria.

If the food was parsimonious the entertainment certainly was not and all sorts and conditions of men, women and children flocked to see the same kind of programme that was provided at Ranelagh until 1803, and went on being offered at Vauxhall until 1859. The lists of singers and instrumentalists means little enough to the average reader today, but all ranks of society enjoyed days out there, however rough the company, in the eighteenth century at least, might be. The famous Dark Walk and Long Alleys caused many an awkward affray, sometimes ending in duels or spontaneous boxing matches. Fireworks did not become a permanent institution at Vauxhall until 1813, having first been introduced as late as 1798; whilst at Ranelagh and other gardens they had for a long time been a popular form of amusement. They went in for a very special treat in 1820 at Vauxhall when Mme Sagin of Paris climbed up a rope to a platform from whence, after a suitable pause to display her spangled dress and helmet with coloured ostrich plumes, she then descended the rope in an explosion of Chinese Fire, described as 'a tempest of fireworks'.

In 1822 the title of The Royal Gardens, Vauxhall was bestowed by a grateful George IV, who had patronised the Gardens so frequently as Prince of Wales. Vauxhall was now turning into a nineteenth century place of entertainment, lit with thousands of oil-lamps, supplying more and more variety shows, equestrian acts, still shows, historical pictures in pavilions and boxes as before but adding an attraction called a Heptaplasiesoptron. This was an effect of revolving glass pillars with ever-changing reflections of the lamps, fountains, palm-trees and twisting snakes. A Sub-marine Cavern replaced the Dark Walk, a Hermit's Cottage on the transparency principle, and a firework tower on which new stunt rope-walkers appeared, imitating Madame Sagin. Indian jugglers, shadow pantomimes, *bals masqués*, comic songs, ballet, and a tendency to vulgarise the shows eventually led to afternoon fêtes and a decline in fortune for the gardens. Gas lamps replaced oil and 1859 saw the last entertainment at Vauxhall, a concert, followed by equestrian acts and dancing. The Fireworks wrote its epitaph across the sky, *Farewell for Ever*.

FAMILY PETS

The love of animals must have started in prehistoric days when the dog became man's best friend and of course the domestic animals were cared for too, like sheep and goats, pigs, hens, ducks and pigeons, horses and donkeys, camels and elephants, if we may include these majestic creatures in our list. Last but not least come the inscrutably beautiful, fastidious, loving cat tribe, who need very special treatment owing to their highly nervous temperament. Lions have been tamed and cheetahs, indeed the list is very long;

Rabbits were popular pets, as we see from this child's plate of *c* 1830. Photograph by Jennifer May.

nor must we leave out mice, rats, squirrels, guinea-pigs, birds, rabbits and of course monkeys. These are by no means all the exotic creatures man has tamed, but for children the number is smaller, as naturally they have to own animals that are not erratic in temperament.

The Chippendale bird-cages show which were some of the easiest of pets to keep, and a visit to the National Gallery or other collections of pictures will immediately give us a veritable menagerie of delightful creatures that have lived amicably in homes.

The little Scottish girl Marjory Fleming* was typical of the children of the past who loved animals. She wrote a letter to her mother when she was six years old saying, 'I saw the most prettyist two tame pidgeons you ever saw and two very wee small kittens like our cat'. She adds later, 'The hawk is in great spirits, it is a nice beast, the gentlest animal that ever was seen. Six canaries, two green linnets and a thrush . . . my aunt lets out the Birds to get the air in her room'. On another occasion she wrote a poem in her journals beginning:

'There is a thing I love to see,
That is our monkey catch a flee,
With looks that shews that he is proud
He gathers round him such a crowd.
But if we scold him he will grin
And up he'll jump and make a din'.

Her best known poem was called Sonnet and written in praise of her pug. Her spelling is characteristic:

'O lovely o most charming pug
Thy graceful air and heavenly mug
The beauties of his mind do shine
And every bit is shaped so fine
Your very tail is most devine
Your teeth is whiter than the snow
Yor are a great buck and a bow
Your eyes are of so fine a shape
More like a christains then an ape
His cheeks is like the roses blume
Your hair is like the ravens plume
His noses cast is of the romen
He is a very pretty weomen
I could not get a ryhme for romen
And was oblidged to call it weomen'.

*See Chapter Six.

This little masterpiece is very well known, but surely bears repeating once more. Obviously the pug was Marjory's best friend in the traditional spirit of children's dogs.

Another child who cherished animals was of course the immortal Beatrix Potter, though her companions whose portraits she painted and whose delightful stories she told were nearly all wild animals. She is so well known that we will be forgiven for only reminding her admirers of those anthropomorphic creatures that have not only pleased readers both young and old all over the world, but have left their portraits on wallpapers, tablecloths, bibs and nursery crockery as well as inspiring a film ballet.

Cats were of course familiar pets in the days of the Pharoahs and so beloved were they that archaeologists have found their mummified bodies lying beside their child owners so that they might go on enjoying each others company in the next world. The cat-who-walked-by-himself of Kipling's story goes to show how frequently

BROTHER, IT'S MY TURN TO RIDE NOW.

A very large family pet dog. Notice the cricket bat. The date of the print is 1789. Photograph by Studio Wreford.

61

the cat has been misunderstood. Their characteristic independence should not be taken for unfriendliness. The chief difference between our two most treasured pets is that the dog has a conscience and knows when he had done wrong. Another difference between the two is the unchanging appearance of cats who have remained more or less similar throughout history. Dogs are far more varied in size and looks. The great majority of nineteenth century French writers loved cats and so did Doctor Johnson, Anatole France, Thomas Hardy, Robert Herrick, William Hogarth, Edward Lear and a whole dictionary of others. The great Mahomet loved his cat so much that once when it lay sleeping nestled against his arm, he preferred to cut off the sleeve of his gown rather than to disturb it. Literature and art are full of references to these mysterious, exquisite pets.

Incidentally, both dogs and cats were worshipped in Ancient Egypt. One of the oldest breeds of dog was the maltese and the tomb of Rameses II held a statuette of one. They also are represented in many portraits of the Renaissance period. Spaniels, with their good tempers and reasonable size have always been considered good safe pets for children. Charles II was devoted to toy spaniels and it is said that he took them to bed with him dressed up as magnificently as he was himself. His father had imported the breed into England giving his name to the black-and-tan King Charles's spaniel.

Birds have been pets also since time immemorial and there are many enchanting portraits of children with their favourites, of which perhaps the picture of James VI of Scotland and I of England carrying his hawk on his hand is the most familiar. Sir Joshua Reynolds painted a boy with his pet owl, but probably the most loved, because the most exotic and affectionate of birds, was the parrot. This long-living pet with its ability to copy our speech has a long history of association with man. Pliny mentions them; and Alexander the Great brought some back from India. The Romans not only kept them as exotic pets but I am sorry to say served them up as table delicacies also. Théophile Gautier, whose passion for cats was renowned, told a story about the one whom he named Madame-Théophile. Asked to look after a friend's parrot he wondered how his cat would behave. She regarded it with profound interest and he interpreted her thoughts like this: 'It is unmistakably a chicken . . . Green though it is, that chicken must be good to eat'. She crawled nearer and nearer the bird's perch and eventually sprang. The parrot, seeing the great danger he was in from this agile creature, unexpectedly called out, 'Have you had your breakfast, Jack?' which filled the cat with unspeakable terror. She decided that the bird with a human voice must be a man, and therefore retreated discomfited beneath her master's bed.

Lord Byron kept a menagerie of undisciplined pets at his villa in Italy at Ravenna. There were peacocks, cranes, monkeys and horses, a falcon and a crow, eight dogs of all sizes and conditions and five cats. Shelley wrote to his second wife when he was visiting Ravenna saying that except for the horses all the animals and birds were free to roam about the house as if they owned it. He added in another letter that the house frequently resounded with their 'unarbitrated quarrels'.

Nurseries in the late nineteenth century were never complete without a canary. These gay little yellow songsters first appeared in Europe in the sixteenth century when the cargo boat in which they travelled was accidentally shipwrecked near Elba. They were rescued and looked after by the islanders, subsequently becoming domesticated throughout Europe. One of the most famous canaries was Toby who belonged to Sir Winston Churchill. He went wherever his master had to go, causing some considerable embarrassment to officials who had to arrange for Toby's visas from the Ministry of Agriculture and a special ticket by air to France on occasions for 'Monsieur Toby'.

CHAPTER FOUR

Children at School

The elderly Dame's school had been the cornerstone of children's learning for a great many years and a 'deaf, poor, patient widow' or a forlorn spinster taught either very young children or those who were unable to go to a boarding-school for financial reasons. Schools had been increasing in the seventeenth and eighteenth centuries but unfortunately English education was inferior to that offered in France and Germany. One might have expected that the formidable Blue Stocking ladies would have had an immediately favourable reaction on all children's learning; but apparently not. The poor unfortunates in Charity Schools were grounded in religious matters but little else. In fact these schools were the result of 'that generous care which several well disposed Persons have taken in the education of Children', wrote Eustace Budgell (1688–1737) a cousin of Addison. A long line of such reformers, differing in both their religious and their social status, helped to educate poor children and collect money for this worthy cause.

In fact there was any amount of goodwill about, but it all seemed to depend on philanthropic efforts of individuals. A follower of the Reverend Griffith Jones, for instance, wrote in the late eighteenth century, 'In divers places throughout England (where there were no Charity Schools) several poor children were taught to read at the expense of the richer inhabitants of the parish'. Jones himself used to spend some of his church collections on hiring and paying teachers. Sometimes the teacher would find somebody to lend a room where he could run a school for two or three months in the summer. The classes were attended by grown-ups as well as children. These 'circulating schools' became famous. The rich Society for Promoting Christian Knowledge was a great help here and not only provided books but aided other 'schools for the poor' besides the circulating ones, thus mixing up religion and education. They had to do this for the very good reason that neither Dissenters nor Catholics were allowed to go to Universities, so both persuasions were forced to train and educate their own ministers or priests.

64

It may surprise some of us to hear that the Society for the Promotion of Christian Knowledge started in 1698. We might well have believed it to have been a nineteenth century institution. Although many schools at this time were either brutal or stupid or both, the Quakers seem to have had excellent schools.

What percentage of the eighteenth century population could read and write is anybody's guess. There were practically no school registers between 1714 and 1815. It is a pretty safe bet to suggest that probably more girls than boys were illiterate, whether they were six or sixty.

By way of contrast it is interesting to consider that a kindergarten type of education was started by a German called Komensky in the seventeenth century. It sounds extraordinarily modern. Komensky taught children through play. They learnt how to make bright-coloured paper baskets, to model clay figures, and weave pretty mats. They sang 'action songs' which taught them about varieties of trades and crafts. As for alphabetical bricks, these useful aids to learning were invented as far back as Elizabethan days, by Sir Hugh Platt, but I suspect the cottage children would have not seen them. Card games for children, amongst them grammatical games, were popular in the seventeenth century too for the patrician child.

Charity Schools had started as early as 1698. Besides teaching poor children to read and write and do simple sums the authorities also clothed them and saw to it that the boys became apprenticed to handcraft types of trade and the girls were prepared for domestic service. Here again the 'benevolence of a few individuals' originated the scheme and nothing more was achieved in promoting popular education until Robert Raikes, a master printer from Gloucester, established the first Sunday School in 1781. Four years after this the Sunday School Society was formed to 'promote by correspondence and pecuniary assistance' the establishment of Sunday Schools. Another job was 'to induce the opulent . . . to visit and superintend them'. Before this it appears that not only the education of the poor was at a remarkably low ebb, but among 'the middle orders' it was not much better, to judge by the bad writing and worse spelling of 'respectable tradesmen' of that period. There was a tendency to think that educating the poor to read, write and be industrious and pious was all that was necessary or indeed advisable. A Scottish traveller called MacRitchie was a clergyman who toured Great Britain and viewed with great disfavour a shepherd sitting on the grass reading a newspaper; whilst a girl in one Charity School reported that a benevolent lady subscriber had been responsible for shutting down her school. The lady had been so shocked at the behaviour of the London poor that she had come to the conclusion that 'they who are born to poverty are born to ignorance and will work harder the less they know . . . She was resolved for her part to spoil no more girls'. Luckily this attitude was not universal, as we have seen at the beginning of this chapter.

Another landmark was the establishment of our first infant schools, pioneered by Robert Owen in 1816. In 1818 a school opened at Brewer's Green, Westminster. The prime movers in this laudable scheme were Brougham, Macauley, Babington Mill and Lord Lansdown. As early as 1808 Joseph Lancaster, who founded

A child's plate celebrating a half-holiday. The boy's clothes date to c 1810. Photograph by Jennifer May.

the British and Foreign Schools Society, had opened an unsectarian Royal Free School in Southwark. By 1828 the indefatigable Mr Brougham was addressing the House of Commons on the bad state of our education and he unfolded his thoughtful proposals for mass instruction, advising that parochial schools should be established and paid for by a small tax on householders, together with 'a trifling weekly payment by the scholars'. It was not quite without strings as the schoolmasters had to be members of the Church of England, insisted Mr Brougham, and moreover they must be chosen by the school rate-payers subject to the approval of the parson. Once more the Dissenters and Catholics were on a sticky wicket, and it is not much of a surprise to hear that the Bill had a mixed reception. But at least it was not wholly without success and an impulse was given to the obligation of educating everybody.

Another good step forward was the appointment of inspectors of factories in 1832 and some strongly worded legislation to protect children. Their education was made compulsory in factories, so that those under eighteen were not to be allowed any more to work at night and no children under nine might work in any factories. The silk mills were exempted for some reason I have not been able to fathom.

Of course we must remember that the Charity Schools' education was heavily weighted in favour of religious and moral instruction advocating humility, industry and contentment. But isn't that better than our present tendency to prefer the psychologically disturbed hooligans to their innocent victims? At least the children did have some sort of education and the Sunday Schools, started in 1780, after tentative beginnings earlier on, offered the same benefits, though only on one day a week, of course.

On 11 April 1846 the *London Illustrated News* printed two drawings of the Lambeth 'Ragged Schools' for girls and for boys, in different rooms. The boys' school shows a large placard on the wall, THOU SHALT NOT STEAL. The boys are all in rags and so are the girls, the teachers have coal-scuttle bonnets and shawls. In fact this scheme was a philanthropic effort to save this forlorn group, who were in too filthy and wretched a condition to be accepted in Charity Schools, and to teach them morality and religion. The schools in the magazine were in Lambeth and opened only on Sunday evenings at 6 o'clock. The year's average attendance was 250 children and 25 teachers. Charles Dickens was an eloquent promoter of this work. I have a pathetic wooden boot, most beautifully carved, the soles gaping and worn out, a mouse peeping through one side and this was used as a collecting box for these poor children.

In 1829 Greville wrote in his famous Diary, 'A new class of reader is produced by the Bell and Lancaster Schools'. These were based on a pupil-teacher system which Flora Thompson mentions is still flourishing in the 1880s. Up to 1833 no public grant was given by Parliament for education and the Charity and Sunday Schools were supported by voluntary subscription. It is rather a shock to our *amour propre* to realise that compulsory education in England only became law in 1876, whereas in Prussia it had been the rule since 1717. The same applied to America in its pre-revolutionary days, when eighteenth century universities were in far from good shape in England with the numbers of undergraduates sadly declining and riots against bad conditions frequent occurrences at public schools like Eton, Winchester and Harrow.

67

A little hamlet on the borders of Oxfordshire and Northampton-shire, called romantically Juniper Hill, was the birth-place in 1876 of a land-labourer's daughter called Flora Thompson. She left school at fourteen and was almost entirely self-taught. In 1939, at sixty-three, her first book *Lark Rise* was published and in 1945, two years before her death, the complete trilogy, called *Lark Rise to Candleford* appeared. Literature and social history are equally indebted to her and she records village life in the transition between the old England of open-fields and largely self-supporting communities with co-operation between neighbours, and the frustrations and heart-burnings of the present, the legacy of the Enclosures* and the Industrial Revolution. In the modern idiom, 'peace and beauty must inevitably give way to progress'. What a tragedy!

However, we are here concerned with the promise of youth, family life and the basic happiness of the landless labourers of the 1870s and 1880s. They still had gardens and were wage-earners in the range of ten shillings a week, (fifty pence). Admittedly they could buy quite a lot with ten shillings then. Eggs cost 20 a shilling; coal was a shilling a hundred-weight. Rents ranged from one shilling to half-a-crown, and some cottages on farms or belonging to small tradesmen were free. The family pig provided bacon for the winter and much more besides; the hens laid eggs, the bees gave honey and sometimes, but not always, a little joint would be roasted on a string in front of the fire on a Sunday. Milk and butter were luxuries, but sugar, lard or treacle went on the bread or butterine, the forerunner of margarine. Country people still made use of hedgerow harvests and garden vegetables and most families kept a pig, some hens and a beehive. The hedges produced crab-apples and sloes, the fields repaid gleaners after harvest time and there were plenty of mushrooms too. The children were healthy in spite of poverty. They enjoyed local amusements like May Day and other traditional festivities. Stable England, with the majority of workers taking pleasure and pride in their work, however, was beginning the transition from the old pattern of country life to the tragedy of today. We see all round us the way the peace and beauty of nature has to give way to 'progress'.

In Flora Thompson's childhood the Industrial Revolution was slowly destroying the old way of life, but it did still linger on. Contentment and a happy life did not depend on riches but on the

*Common land which came under the plough according to the Enclosure Acts.

little everyday things and those small joys were recorded faithfully by this enchanting self-taught girl of the 1880s.

At Lark Rise, she tells us, the only shop they boasted was kept in the back kitchen of the Inn, a general store of the type that surprisingly still exists today in outlying hamlets. As a child just after the first World War I remember such a shop, a ten-minutes scramble along a path across the common from my artist uncle's cottage. The shop was reminiscent of the one kept by the sheep in *Alice Through the Looking Glass*. The greatest temptation was a ha'porth of striped humbugs in a paper cornet weighed out from a bottle marked 'Play up Rovers'. All those small pleasures my friends and I shared with Flora Thompson, as we gathered cowslips and bluebells, primroses and later on dog-roses from the hedges and brought home tiddlers or tadpoles in jam jars. We would spend hours waiting to see the rabbits come out of their holes or the hares wildly scamper about on their mad March courtships; or we watched the water-birds on the ponds, and the frogs and the toads and newts.

The Lark Rise children came in families of eight or ten and managed to pack into one or two bedrooms like sardines in a tin, the boys often sleeping downstairs or even with childless neighbours. Everybody lived a great part of their lives out of doors, which seems to have kept them healthy. The word 'nerves' or 'nervy', as we use them today, were unknown, despite the over-crowded homes. The children of course picked up country lore rather than book-learning and knew all the names of local birds and flowers and trees.

Flora Thompson used to play games with broken crockery and stones and moss, making houses, or in the winter building snowmen and sliding along the lanes. Her generation, that played the old traditional games like Oranges and Lemons, London Bridge and Here come Three Tinkers, was perhaps the last one to play them spontaneously amongst themselves. Ring games like *Green Gravel* date many years into past history, as do *Poor Mary is a-weeping* and *How many miles to Babylon*; this last at Lark Rise was translated to Banbury Town, which was not far off. The games of skipping, marbles, hopscotch and spin-tops were popular. School for these children was a mile and half's walk away and they had to have their breakfast at 7 o'clock so as to reach school by 9 o'clock. There was no traffic problem then and only the farmer's gig or the brewer's dray to churn up the white dust, and sometimes the smart four-in-hand of the local Squire came spanking by.

The school was a large classroom and about 45 children attended.

The school-mistress does not seem to have been inspiring, but poor soul she was expected to teach all the classes at the same time, with the help of two children of about 12 years old, who had been at the school and were now earning a shilling a week by helping their former school-mistress in her duties. Reading and writing was just about all the children ever learnt, with a sprinkling of bible lore and sums. Of course the majority of children in England, especially the boys, left school by the time they were twelve.

The Village School, *c* 1840. Engraving by H. Bourne after T. Webster. Courtesy of the British Museum.

This idyllic picture, remember, is childhood in the country. The town-dwellers were not so lucky, but by the time Flora Thompson was growing up there was a universal interest in promoting education for everybody and we can safely say that there was no looking back from that time onwards.

SOME BOARDING SCHOOLS FOR BOYS

The tendency to lump all public schools together is misleading. In fact the aims of their founders were as diverse as the school buildings. They represented all kinds of religion and all sorts of boys, from the original design to train poor scholars at Winchester and other early foundations, to the much more liberal outlook and intake of boys which has developed today. Rugby, Harrow and Shrewsbury went on for longer supporting 'the poor and indigent' but Eton, Westminster and Winchester as early as the seventeenth century were beginning to teach only the rich and the aims of their fourteenth and fifteenth century founders were forgotten. Originally education was connected closely with the Church, whether Catholic or Protestant. Then came the eighteenth and early nineteenth century emphasis on rewards to the strong and a systematic 'licking

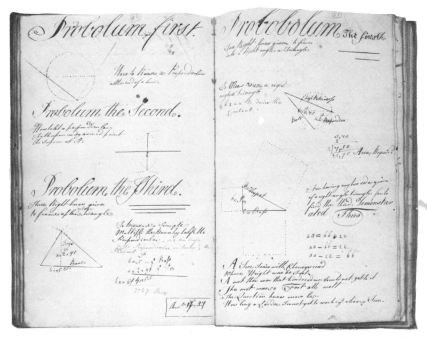

A boy, aged 12, owned this exercise book dated 1760. It is bound in vellum and the cover reads 'John Keale is my name, England is my nation, in Tedford I was born, withern is my habitation—don't steal this book for fear of shame, for Hear (sic) you find the Owner's name John Keale'. Photograph by Studio Wreford.

into shape' of the wretched scholars, teaching by blows rather than by persuasion so that the continual feuds between boys and masters resulted eventually in frequent rebellions. There were no less than four rebellions at Winchester between 1770 and 1793 for example.

Westminster, in the 1770s, was a good school, and there Mr Parker of Saltram sent his son Jack. The boy started his school life at a day-school in Plymouth, getting up at 6 o'clock and walking there 'with great resolution and good humour'. Then he was sent to a preparatory school at Hammersmith, which was luckily good too; and indeed it *was* luck, as no school inspectors existed in those days. After public school Jack went to the University. Boys in the eighteenth century went there at the age of 15 or 16 and lived it up in the way of all undergraduates before or since, idling and drinking, 'smoking', shouting abuse at the Dean, 'being in beer' and sitting up to the small hours.

Little James and George Russell, a 100 years earlier, went to Westminster and set up a family tradition. Even then it was customary for fathers to send their sons to the schools where they themselves had been educated.

The man who had an enormous influence on public school and indeed general education was the famous Dr Thomas Arnold, who was born in 1795 and elected headmaster of Rugby in 1827. One of his testimonials was prophetic. It read, 'if Mr Arnold were elected . . . he would change the face of education all through the public schools of England'. He appears to have done just that. He took over when these schools were at an extremely low ebb. By virtue of his remarkable personality he succeeded in giving back to education the basis of religion and the right of the boys to self-government, guiding them to this end through the headmaster and his staff, and putting idealism in front of them as an aim instead of the maxim that might is right. Of course he chose his staff with the greatest care requiring 'first, religious and moral principles, secondly gentlemanly conduct, thirdly intellectual ability'. All these virtues were also to be those the boys were to be trained to absorb. All his life he was concerned with putting precepts into practise, which religion seemed to him so seldom to do.

He introduced the prefect system and what he called the duty of criticism. Of course we have only to read *Tom Brown's Schooldays* to see that he upheld discipline by flogging, but we must not forget that he took over an extremely unruly mob, and his severity was certainly tempered with justice. Before he came the rule was by fear and punishment, with the weak and timorous inevitably suffering for the rest of their lives. The old cliché of 'a brute but a just brute' was at first possibly as fair a comment on him as on his successor Dr Temple, for whom it was coined.

The poet Matthew Arnold, the eldest of Dr Arnold's nine children, described his father as one 'fervent, heroic and good, Helper and friend of mankind'. Certainly this great headmaster restored confidence in our educational system with his emphasis on truth, honesty and kindness. He seems to have inspired devotion and loyalty in his pupils. Loyalty, as Rex Warner so concisely points out 'is a fine quality, but as we have seen in our own times, of no absolute value unless associated with intelligence and principle'.

72

That was the definition given to this misused word by Arnold. Moreover he detested the idea of a sense of honour rather than a sense of duty. That keynote of the late nineteenth century public schools 'chivalry' was anathema to Arnold. He equated it with the name of Anti-Christ, 'the more detestable for the very guise of the Archangel ruined, which has made it so seductive to the most generous spirits—but to me so hateful because it is in direct opposition to the impartial justice of the Gospel and its comprehensive feeling of equal brotherhood; and because it so fostered a sense of honour rather than a sense of duty'. Brutus, you remember, was an honourable man.

Arnold combined respect for the past with the reformer's zeal for innovations. He died in 1842. A certain stagnation during the next sixty years caused A. C. Benson to write rather caustically in 1904, 'I declare that it makes me very sad sometimes to see these well-groomed, rational, manly boys all taking the same view of things, all doing the same things, smiling politely at the eccentricity of anyone who finds matter for serious interest in books, in art or music'. This perfectly valid criticism of that period shows the beginning of the swing of the pendulum again; but the twentieth century had started and this new spirit of change has no place here where we have chosen to deal with matters concerning the eighteenth and nineteenth centuries.

The great day schools were grammar schools with many of them boasting considerably older foundations even than Winchester and Eton. They, like Arnold, were concerned with the building of character as much as that of intellectual achievements. They catered for 'a mixture of boys from various stations'.

If King Alfred founded the first public school at Wantage to educate the sons of the nobility, the Middle Ages saw a huge number of grammar schools being founded, training boys for professions. In medieval days nobody thought of universal education. We have to thank the Puritans and later the sects like Presbyterians, Baptists, Quakers, Congregationalists, Unitarians and later on the Methodists for that idea. In fact the commonwealth saw great increase in seats of education when at least 50 new grammar schools were founded. The pattern was for Eton, Winchester, Harrow and Westminster to attract the nobility, and other old schools and grammar schools to cater for local boys, the 'middling' classes and the tradesmen and yeomen. No *system* of education existed and any good teacher could open and maintain a private school. Compulsory education is only a 100 years old today.

In the eighteenth century most rich men's sons first learnt their lessons at home from a tutor. Then they went to a boarding school. Creevey quotes one boy at a school at Hackney as saying that 'the habit of swearing was so inveterate I never got rid of it'. The inevitable bullying, not to mention flogging, was under severe criticism even then, but it persisted all too long.

Foreigners like François de la Rochefoucauld and a German visiting England in 1782 were, on the other hand, much impressed by what they considered to be our broadminded approach to education. They saw it of course from the outside. The German liked the natural appearance of our English boys, pointing out that six-year-old Berliners were still dressed like adults in lace-trimmed coats and little swords, their long hair restrained in enormous hair-nets. English boys at this time wore open-breasted shirts and short hair till they were eighteen or more. The young German may not have read Dr Johnson's severe declaration that in school, 'Severity must be continued until obstinacy be subdued and negligence be cured'. The Doctor died in 1784. Westminster had been under the domination of that famous lover of the birch Dr Busby most of the seventeenth century and in the eighteenth century Dr Markham followed his example, though Westminster retained its excellent reputation for scholarship despite vice and corruption. By and large, however, the eighteenth century was a period of decline in education, of rule by terror and frequent school rebellions. Westminster, originally founded for 'the poor and indigent' like Eton and Winchester, now was filled with the sons of rich fathers who were ready to pay.

At Norwich High School Mr Jones numbered amongst his pupils William and Horatio Nelson. Horatio was born in 1758 and one of his schoolfellows wrote to him years later, 'I well remember where you sat in the schoolroom . . . between the parlour door and the chimney . . . we were under the lash of Classic Jones . . . as keen a flogger as merciless Busby'. Incidentally it is interesting to reflect that both these boys would have spoken with the strong twang of their Norfolk dialect.

Eton in the eighteenth century educated such boys as William Pitt, Henry Fielding, Arne, who composed Rule Britannia, Earl Howe of Ushant and 'the glorious victory of the first of June' 1794; not to mention Wellington, Charles James Fox and Canning as well as Horace Walpole, Gray and many others. In 1809 the fearsome Keate began his reign over the boys. In fairness to these formidable headmasters one has to remember that there was a chronic shortage of teachers at the time. At Charterhouse, for instance, in 1821 there were only five masters for 431 boys, and this was nothing new. Shrewsbury in 1798 had been reduced to only two pupils and so at least the new headmaster appointed then had no boys or teachers to put a spanner in the works of his task of rebuilding the school and only the memory of tradition to back him up.

In the nineteenth century the home was ruled by an all-powerful Papa backed up by an outwardly frail and fluttering Mamma with a hidden strength of character that heralded the early rumblings from the era of the equal rights for women.

Horrible innovations like cold baths became popular and it was a great age for 'improving' the minds of the young. A little verse from one book is sufficient to point the trend.

'Would you like to be told the best use for a penny?
I can tell you a use which is better than any;
Not on toys or on fruit or on sweetmeats to spend it,
But over the seas to the heathen to send it!'

A wretched little boy home for the holidays from Harrow and one might have hoped now free to enjoy a little fun and games addresses his sister's governess. 'Madam', says this unnatural paragon, 'I shall esteem myself much obliged to you for permitting me to partake of your instruction'. Amongst this boy's schoolfellows was George Gordon, Lord Byron. I wonder what he would have said to the governess.

This was the era of Dr Keate at Eton, who birched his scholars in batches of twenty or more on occasion. Did school begin at 6 o'clock at Eton as it did at the same period at Dulwich? There the teachers very sensibly stayed in bed until nine and admitted their pupils into their bedroom at six to repeat their lessons. This school was founded as early as Shakespeare's day by Edward Alleyn (1566–1626) who was an actor. The boys admitted in those days to the college were required to be twelve poor scholars, who shared the advantages of education with a master and a warden, four fellows, six poor brothers and six poor sisters.

This seems a good moment to look at girls' education and schools, and to see what was happening to the girls whilst their brothers faced the rigours of boarding school. The jollity of universities and the excitement of a grand tour we shall hear about later.

AGAINST ACCOMPLISHMENTS

Dr Johnson was not much taken with Hannah More. 'She does not gain upon me, Sir', he said, 'I think her empty-headed'. Her excessive flattery of the great man on their first meeting, in which she appears to have been insensible of his increasing annoyance at her fulsome praise, must have prejudiced him against her. As she was a dear friend of Horace Walpole, it is not likely that she would have pleased the Doctor. Walpole would have liked her effusive manner. When he wrote to her, 'Dear holy Hannah', he meant this affectionately and not as a sneer.

One of the most forceful of the group of eighteenth century Blue Stockings, or more familiarly Blues, Hannah More was born in 1745. When she was fifty she wrote a book called *Strictures on the Modern System of Female Education*. It was long overdue. Women, according to Addison, needed only to study 'ornamental subjects' in order to pursue their only function, to 'allure and shine' for the sole purpose of attracting a rich and preferably noble husband. Hannah More, Lady Mary Wortley Montagu and others amongst the many beautiful, colourful and intelligent women of the age, wanted girls to be trained neither as 'Amazons nor as Circassians' but as 'rational and accountable beings'. Here was the voice of Women's Lib talking to her sisters of today across 200 years.

When we think of the long line of young Victorian girls who spent half a lifetime turning out those admittedly charming 'ornamental studies', learning to dance a little, play a little on the pianoforte and sing, draw a little and sew a great deal, we forget how pioneers of female education were striving in the eighteenth and nineteenth centuries to break down the fetters which bound their sisters to a domesticated life of child-bearing and 'accomplishments'.

Hannah More was in this case talking of the leisured classes of her times, and she also looked back to 'our great-grandmothers who distinguished themselves by truly substantial tent-work, chairs and carpets, by needlework pictures of Solomon and the Queen of Sheba'. She consigned all the arts of clothwork, crape-work, chenille-work, wafer-work and ribbon-work to perdition and asked the question, what is the true educational value of accomplishments? Well, Hannah, not much perhaps, but in our own day of dying crafts and education for everybody which you helped us to win, we are less angry about their small value and collect avidly those 'ornamental studies' of the past.

In those days, however, we must remember that Fanny Burney was overcome and reduced to tears at the idea of anybody knowing she had written a novel; that neither Jane Austen nor the Brontës felt their books would be received so well coming from the female pen and therefore chose male pseudonyms, whilst Henry Fielding's sister Sarah, a good deal earlier than these novelists, as she was born in 1710, published her first book anonymously. It was difficult for intelligent women to swim against the tide.

Hannah More, therefore, was all for bracing the girls to take a more intellectual diet in their studies. Queen Charlotte obviously agreed with her as she and her daughters read a great number of serious, heavy books and discussed them with each other and their friends. Hannah More saw to it that all classes were catered for as she wrote also stories for 'Persons of the Middle Rank' so that soon the milliners and dressmakers were reading passages out loud to each other of a more or less improving nature.

The female version of Lord Chesterfield and his letters to his son were numerous in the eighteenth century. In fact there was a great urge for self-expression in verse or letters, the fashion being to address poetic effusions to rather painfully romantic Florizels, Damons, Amandas and so forth. One poem was entitled 'verses composed and sung with a Sweet Voice by a lady to her Husband a few minutes before she Died'. Nobody thought this in the least funny. Letters, usually love-letters, were mostly sent to discarded mistresses or young noblemen. The Blues, however, wrote to instruct and advise. One of the most celebrated female letter-writers was Mrs Hester Chapone whose *Letters on the Improvement of the Mind, addressed to a young Lady* appeared in 1773. She was born earlier than Hannah More, in 1727 and was a 'dear and life-long friend of Johnson'. For ten brief months she was the wife of a London attorney. Her letters breathe out warmth and affection. She writes to her niece with sense and sincerity, natural piety and a good moral attitude. Quite an army of Blues ladies, much to Dr Johnson's satisfaction, were writing letters in the vein of Swift and Madame de Sévigné and they had great influence on their readers. Some of the correspondents were addressing real-life daughters or nieces whilst others were writing to imaginary characters. The letter-writing tradition was carried on by Fanny Burney in her masterpiece *Evelina* which is entirely made up of correspondence.

In her advice on education Mrs Chapone gave pride of place to history with geography and chronology to back up the study. She also advocated the teaching of French. Her letters form a sort of post-graduate course of reading for girls from the age of 15. Self-education was the keynote, with an emphasis on training the memory to store all the facts gleaned in the innumerable books that were recommended reading. Mrs Chapone laid the usual stress on the moral aspects of her subjects. She advised the favourite niece, to whom she addressed her letters, to study all the historical plays of Shakespeare, Milton's *Paradise Lost* and translations of Homer and Virgil. Letter-writing developed into such a popular pastime in the eighteenth century that schools paid much attention to clear handwriting and epistolatory skill. Models recommended to girls were Pope's letters, Pliny's letters in translation, but best of all those of Madame de Sévigné.

Meanwhile the daughters of George III were taught not only to read serious books but also 'a thousand ingenious uses of the needle' by a talented French lady. A school of the period kept by a Mrs Voysey at Salisbury in 1778 was also teaching accomplishments to her young ladies. Wood-carving, engraving and turnery went side by side with 'Fillagree, Steel and Varnish Work' as well as wax flower-making and cut-paper work. It was these last that the women writers like Mary Wollstonecraft, Maria Edgeworth and Hannah More disliked so much. Mrs Delany, that much-loved friend of the Royal Family and of Fanny Burney, must have had her reservations about these revolutionary ideas as she herself was a great adept at cut-paper 'mosaicks' as she called her own special version of the art, and she excelled at all the parlour pastimes. She, however, was born in 1740, living to be a very old lady of 88 when she died, active to the last; so she was a survival of the bad old days as far as the blue-stocking ladies were concerned.

Luckily the Court approved of intellectual pursuits, even though they were not highly intellectual themselves. Queen Charlotte read works by those erudite ladies Hannah More and Mrs Trimmer besides seeing that her daughters learnt the harpsichord and other arts. In this she was lucky to be supported by her husband, as the late King George II was always put in a transport of rage at the sight of books and his wife had to read hers secretly in her closet.

One thing is certain. Education for either sex even in the so-called educated classes was at a fairly low level in the eighteenth century if we believe Dean Swift, who, incidentally, was a great friend and admirer of Mrs Delany. In 1765 he was writing, 'Out of fifteen thousand families of lords and estated gentlemen one in thirty is tolerably educated; the daughters of great and rich families are left entirely to their ignorant mothers; or they are sent to boarding schools or put into the hands of English or French governesses'.* He added that they generally chose the worst governesses they could get for their money.

Boarding schools for girls in the eighteenth century were not only mostly inferior but their influence was often actually corrupting. I have a book entitled *The Boarding School Romps* published in the late eighteenth century as a harlequinade book. Obviously a great deal was learnt about philandering with dubious 'Rakes and

*Works of Johnathan Swift.

78

Bloods' if nothing else. As for the school mistresses they were often drawn from the ranks of the unfortunate, the impecunious or even the adventuress. Elopements from boarding schools were frequent. Some of the schools were good, however, and did not necessarily pander to fashions of the moment only and the learning of more and more 'accomplishments'.

When Sarah Fielding wrote her delightful children's story of *The Governess, or the Little Female Academy* in 1748 her setting is a country boarding school, with a charming background of arbours of roses and honeysuckle in the garden and girls running in the fields and eating curds and cream. In 1780 the cathedral town of Salisbury had three girls' schools. One kept by a Miss Read in 1797 taught 'all sorts of needlework, tambour, etc., and the strictest attention paid to morals'. This included 'Board and Education, Music, Writing and Accompts (sic), Dancing and the French and English languages'. Mrs Voysey's school in 1788 was perhaps a little grander as she charged an entrance fee of £1 11s 6d to Miss Read's one guinea. The third school was founded by the brother of Sidney, Earl of Godolphin, Lord High Treasurer of Great Britain, who left money to found a school in his Will. In 1784 the Godolphin School, still going strong today, was opened to admit 'eight young orphan gentlewomen with fortunes under £900'.

Another class of school in the eighteenth century was the group conducted by refugees from the French Revolution. Mrs Sherwood* was sent to one at Reading. Both men and women teachers were employed and there were about 60 girls. After the execution of Louis XVI there was quite a rush of French emigrants to Reading, so that the school became more like a hospitable château than a seat of learning, with dances in the Abbey garden and unlimited hospitality offered to the noble *émigrées*.

Once we reach the nineteenth century however, the progress of women's education was unbroken even if at the start to be sure, the picture is gloomy.

The educational acts of 1870, 1903 and 1918 were milestones in which it was established that the elementary schoolgirl's education must be inseparable from that of the schoolboy. It was to be her right to benefit from instruction and she was to be the charge of the nation equally with her brother. The founding of a Governesses' Benevolent Institution in 1848 was to lead on to more attempts to better the lot of that badly paid and struggling class of woman. The same year Queen's College in London was opened as a non-resident

*Who wrote The Fairchild Family.

college for women as well as Bedford College. In 1862 a few girls were allowed to take the Oxford and Cambridge local examinations. The famous Miss Buss and Miss Beale started Cheltenham Girls School and other schools of equal importance followed. Henceforward 'accomplishments' in the old sense of the word took second place.

CHAPTER FIVE

Governesses

The ubiquitous governess, sometimes teased and bullied but also appreciated and loved, was holding sway in English homes over a large number of upper class children who survived infancy. So great indeed was her reputation that in the nineteenth century she was also reigning over continental schoolrooms. In fact the faithful creature seems to have been like a missionary, carrying the flag of her profession all over the world. We can boast that during the nineteenth century, England exported some of the best nannies and governesses available.

In Plantagenet days, French and English were essential languages for any family aspiring to high places at Court. Ladies were appointed to look after the royal and noble families, and generally they themselves were from high ranking families, too. The children were looked after entirely by the governesses, who even controlled the tutors and saw to the well-being both physical and mental of their charges.

The first governess, in the present sense of the word, who was given a salary for her exacting job, was Mistress Hamblyn. In company with Mrs Anne Mantell, the 'olde Governess' of Sir Philip Sidney's sister, she probably received 'twentie poundes' for her wages. The impoverished, but kind and gentle, Mistress Hamblyn taught the Sherrington girls their lessons at Lacock Abbey in Tudor days.* In the early eighteenth century we find an outstanding governess, who began her career when most of us would have been looking forward to a quiet retirement. Having written rather a solemn book, when she was twenty-six in 1709, entitled *An English Saxon Homily on the Birthday of St Gregory*, her friends called her 'the Saxon Lady'. The Dodo's story in '*Alice*' comes to mind at this formidable title. 'What is the driest thing you know?' Elizabeth Elstob later opened a small school to save herself from the workhouse, and this she kept with some success, but little emoluments. When she was 53 she met the sister of Mrs Pendarves, who

*See Bea Howe's *A Galaxy of Governesses*.

later became famous as Mrs Delany. In spite of her efforts to find Elizabeth Elstob more congenial and paying work than her village school, nothing came of it as Elizabeth felt unwilling to accept a position teaching rich children rather than poor ones. At last, thanks to the future Mrs Delany's continued efforts on her behalf, at the age of 55 she accepted the post of governess to the children of the Duchess of Portland, arriving at Bulstrode in 1739. Here she lived in the isolated schoolroom, ignored by the Duchess and her friends to a great extent, but perfectly happy teaching her 'charming little Ladies' from dawn to dusk. She loved children and remained devoted to her pupils until 1753, when Mrs Delany wrote and told her sister that Mrs Elstob was in failing health, and in June 1956 she died.

This governess was a brilliant scholar, who was born before the time when women were to be recognised as intellectuals and encouraged in their learning. She had to swallow the same bitter pill as Fanny Burney took some 50 years later; that is to say they both learnt that the great ladies of the eighteenth century were more interested in social behaviour than in women's education, even though this was the period when the schoolroom first took its place beside the nursery and playroom in English homes.

One advantage the eighteenth century governess had over the nineteenth century one was that it was considered to be the height of bad manners to be rude to or slight the governess. By the end of that century, there were French emigrant ladies ready to accept 40 guineas a year for the security of a home with food and laundry thrown in. Sometimes they earned 50 or 60 guineas. After all, a governess might be expected to look after the whole of a large household whilst the parents were travelling abroad or in London. The responsibility was great, and the governesses were treated affectionately and kept for the rest of their lives, if need arose, with the family.

Now we will look at some governesses in greater depth, and where better can we start than with Sarah Fielding, clever sister of a brilliant brother.

SARAH FIELDING
1710–1768

In England the word governess has but one meaning; 'a female teacher, especially of children, in a private household'. In France the word has no less than three different meanings: the wife of a Governor, the woman who is responsible for the education of one or several children, and thirdly, a lady looking after the household of either a bachelor or a widower. Here, of course, we are concerned with the English term, but in the eighteenth century a governess did not only take up duties in a private household. She might be the owner of a Female Academy. Sarah Fielding, sister of Henry Fielding, author of *Tom Jones*, published a book in 1749. It was called *The Governess, or Little Female Academy*. The story was about the widow of a clergyman. She was called, appropriately enough, Mrs Teachum and she had under her wing nine girls between the ages of twelve and fourteen. The Academy's principal aim was 'to improve their (the girls') minds in all useful knowledge; to render them obedient to their superiors and gentle, kind and affectionate to one another'. What could be better than that?

The book appears to be based very much on happenings in Sarah Fielding's own life. She was born in 1710 into a small landowning family with some aristocratic ancestors. There were six living children in the family and they resided at East Stour in Dorset. At the age of seven Sarah lost her mother and she and her brothers and sisters were looked after by a maternal great-aunt. Their father re-married a year later a Roman Catholic and this caused endless family discussions. So Henry Fielding was sent off to Eton and the three eldest girls went to a boarding school in Salisbury, run by a Mrs Mary Rookes, where they learnt 'to work and read and write and to talk French and Dance and be brought up as Gentlewomen'. Sarah was therefore able to write from first hand experience about a 'Little Female Academy'. One incident about the man with the raree show, a travelling peep-show★, must certainly have happened to Sarah herself. Rather sanctimoniously she remarks how the Parish children enjoyed this entertainment, but she, at the tender age of six, thought reading more worth while than 'to lose my time at such foolish entertainments'. The love of reading she shared with brother Henry, three years her elder. Henry refers to books like the chap-book tales of *Guy of Warwick* and *Jack the Giant-Killer* in his own books, and probably they also enjoyed *Robinson Crusoe*, published in 1719 when Sarah was nine, and seven years later *Gulliver's Travels*.

Like so many other spinsters of the eighteenth century, when she grew up poor Sarah found herself dependent on male relations for her upkeep since there were few ways of acquiring 'a genteel maintenance' for women. She did, however, have the talent and the spirit to publish anonymously a first book in May 1744, and it was thought by many that, in spite of Henry Fielding's foreword attri-

★See Oxford Dictionary of the Theatre on these shows and also Chapter III of this book.

83

G

buting it to 'a young woman', it was really by himself. *David Simple* went into a second edition. In this picaresque novel, *The Adventures of David Simple in Search of a Faithful Friend*, the heroine, Cynthia, shares her authoress's passion for reading. In fact, Sarah made reference to no less than 60 authors in her own four novels, besides her brother Henry's works, Shakespeare, Milton, the Bible and Montaigne, Pope, Horace and Virgil. She was a very well-read young woman. In 1748 Sarah read the proofs of *The Governess* and in January 1749 it was published, in the same year as her brother's *History of Tom Jones, a Foundling*. The two books sold well, and Sarah's bookseller probably recognised a winner when he saw one and not only bought the copyright but planned a second cheaper edition for August 1749.

The Governess is notable as the first novel written for children and she too was writing for amusement as well as instruction; but she, like other writers of her age, believed in having a moral purpose for her books. She was strongly opposed to birching children, which was a very common form of correction; and also she was, like her brother and Samuel Richardson, against cruelty to animals. Don't forget that the little boarding school of Sarah's educational novel and her own experience was a democratic establishment. Most villages boasted one or two of these schools where 'Miss, whose mamma sells oysters, tells Miss, whose papa deals in small coal, that her governess shall know it if she spits in her face or does anything else unbecoming a lady'.* The ale-house keeper, the shoe-maker, the blacksmith as well as the country gentleman's daughter all enjoyed the same education if they could pay for it. Lower middle-class parents were trying to better themselves and the eighteenth century was always ready to accept people for what they were rather than for what family they sprang from.

Later on such private schools were not all of the same high standard as the *Little Female Academy*. Charlotte Brontë and Charles Dickens are only two of the many authors who point out the way pupils could be exploited by the unscrupulous. Sarah's Mrs Teachum provided writing, taught by a visiting writing-master, reading, gardening, needlework and all 'proper forms of Behaviour'. She also encouraged her pupils to 'run in the Fields and to gather Flowers' and go for walks of two or three miles in the pleasant countryside which we now are watching sadly as it diminishes.

Charlotte Yonge, who was born in 1823, chose *The Governess* as one of her favourite books. Indeed she included it in an anthology

*Quoted in *English Life in the Eighteenth Century*, ed. G. A. Sambrook, 1955.

84

of stories she published in 1870, called *A Storehouse of Stories*. Mrs Sherwood, some years earlier, also singled it out as a good book for children and the redoubtable Mrs Sarah Trimmer, writing about her childhood reading in the 1790s mentions *The Governess* as one amongst the few books she and her brother had to read.

The history of Mrs Teachum, therefore, and her 'nine Girls with their nine days Amusement' became the pattern for others to follow and stories about school life both for girls and boys followed one another from that day to this and will no doubt interest children as long as there are schools.

SELINA TRIMMER
1765–1829

Selina's mother, Mrs Sarah Trimmer, wrote a book that was famous in her time, called *The History of the Robins*. This little book for children was designed to encourage the little dears to be kind to animals. It was one of the earliest of its kind. In fact, Mrs Trimmer was no mean writer, and she very sensibly brought up her eldest daughter to look after the education of her younger children whilst she herself, in common with a whole regiment of other gifted ladies, wrote books to help children to learn both their lessons and good moral behaviour. Mrs Trimmer's views were firm, but she had a belief in original sin. Children, she was persuaded, were born wicked. *The Story of the Robins*, first published in 1786 as *Fabulous Histories*, has considerable charm as a period piece; but her intention was not to amuse so much as 'to convey moral instruction'. She called the baby robins, Dicky, Flopsy and Pecksy, and later on 'woodcuts by Bewick' in the 1821 edition, added to the attraction of the tale. The book was dedicated to Her Royal Highness Princess Sophia on 'Nov. 3, 1785'.

The opening sentences of the first chapter promise well; 'In a hole which time had made in a wall covered with ivy, a pair of Redbreasts built their nest'. Harriet and Frederick feed the birds but Mrs Trimmer has to remind the children that 'there are poor people as well as poor birds'. Later, one of the robins remarks piously, 'Forgive me, dear mother, I will not again offend you'. Nevertheless, what a picture of life in Georgian days it gives, for the robin family are exactly like their human counterparts. Robin is the pushing young particle and Dicky tends to be a bit timid. Pecksy is the good girl, an example to us all, presenting a luscious spider to her parents as a tribute to their toils and fatigue bringing up the chicks. The fledglings also have to be protected against unsuitable friends. 'I cautioned him repeatedly not to make acquaintance with the sparrows . . .'. They even have to learn accomplishments, and their father unctuously reminds them to 'apply yourselves to whatever your mother requires of you: she is an excellent judge both of your talents and of what is suitable to your station in life'. How odd that Mrs Trimmer was violently opposed to fairy stories. Her bird-characters would grace any of them. She certainly did not intend them to make us laugh.

In her periodical *The Guardian of Education* (1802–1804) Mrs Trimmer made her famous attack on fairy stories, with particular venom directed to *Cinderella*. She stormed at its theme of 'envy, jealousy and dislike for mothers-in-law (meaning stepmothers) and half-sisters, vanity, a love of dress, etc.'. One excellent invention she must be credited with, however, and that is teaching by pictures, designed to be displayed on nursery walls with explanatory booklets for the teacher's use. These prints, published about 1787, were an immediate success and were referred to as her 'Descriptions'. Reading Madame de Genlis's *Adèle et Théodore* gave her the idea.

Like Mrs Sherwood, Selina's celebrated mother believed in the sternest piety and also, sadly, in the tendency of children to choose the evil course rather than the good. Well, perhaps she was right if she meant by it that children usually enjoy the excitement of being naughty more than the virtue of being good.

Against this background of home influences, with everything orderly and regulated, Selina was brought up and in her turn brought up her younger brothers and sisters. The Dowager Lady Spencer, whose daughter Georgiana was married to the Duke of Devonshire, decided that nobody could be more suitable than her old friend's well-brought-up daughter Selina, to be put in charge of the remarkable collection of children in the Devonshire House nursery. One of the children, Caroline Ponsonby, that arch-poseuse, later to be the bane of Byron's life as well as that of her poor husband William Lamb, jotted down a few notes on her childhood. The children's meals she said were 'served on silver in the morning and (they) carried their own plates down at night and believed the world to be divided between Dukes and beggars'. She added that 'we had no idea that bread and butter was made, how it came we did not pause to think . . . My kind Aunt Devonshire had taken me when my mother's ill-health prevented my being at home'.

Selina's tribe of children requiring education in this curious Whig household consisted of the Duchess's two daughters, Georgiana and Harriet, and the baby Hartington, the Bessborough's three boys and their sister Caroline, very wild and untamed; Lady Elizabeth Foster's two boys by her estranged husband, and Augustus Clifford, Caroline St Jules and Eliza, about whose parentage there was a veil drawn, though the two elder children bore a strong resemblance to Lady Elizabeth. They were in fact her children by the Duke of Devonshire. Many French refugees from the Terror joined the household, as the hospitable doors of Devonshire House were open as a haven to them. Selina, therefore, also had French children added to the dozen regular members of her nursery, amongst them Corisande de Gramont and her sister and their brother the Duc de Guiche.

The unusual *ménage à trois* living at Devonshire House consisted of the fifth Duke himself, the Duchess, gifted with all the charm in the world, and Lady Elizabeth Foster, daughter of Lord Bristol and wife of an Irish squire. The Duchess had married her cousin in 1774 when she was only seventeen and the marriage was an arrangement that Lord Spencer her father had made for her. Her dissolute grandfather, Jack Spencer was the adored grandson of the fiery Sarah Jennings, Duchess of Marlborough. Georgiana was tall with chestnut hair and dark blue eyes and she may have inherited some of her beauty and temperament from Sarah. This, combined with a vivid complexion, a splendid figure and unbounded vitality gave her a personality which conquered many hearts. The Duke was grave, phlegmatic and rather old-fashioned with formal courteous manners. He liked routine which Georgiana certainly was incapable of giving him, and his one passion was gambling. This taste they did share, unfortunately. William went to the club whilst Georgiana entered into the gay life of London Society. Her two intimate friends, whom she made within the first two years of her cool *mariage de convenance* were Lady Melbourne and Charles James Fox. It was a world Selina Trimmer knew nothing about. Her world was the nursery schoolroom.

The Duchess kept no routine and her doors, as we have seen, were open to all comers provided they were witty, amusing conversationalists and enjoyed gambling. She was probably one of those people whose presence disarms criticism but whose absence often reminds her acquaintances of her shortcomings. Selina had been warned about Georgiana's fatal charm by Lady Spencer, who had engaged her as a sort of watch-dog over her beloved grandchildren and wished them to be brought up as simply as her own children had been. She wanted them to be steeped in a proper respect for tradition and good behaviour. Selina, who was only twenty-one, cannot have found life very easy in the Devonshire family, in spite of the collection of books her mother had recommended and the terrestrial globes and other familiar objects with which she surrounded herself. She was protected of course by her impeccable standards and good sense, but she knew only too well what a rackety life her employers led. The beautiful Duchess gave her complete authority over the children. Her position was strictly only governess to the two little girls, Georgiana and Harriet. The other children were thrown in for good measure.

The Duchess loved her children and kept in touch with Selina by letter when, as frequently happened, she was away. One of Selina's early letters in the summer of 1789 referred to 'dear Lady Harriet' for whom she admitted partiality as being a most 'promising child; she is in high spirits at being the Queen of the Day and directing it with all kind of droll ideas'. It was Harriet's fourth birthday. Her mother was meanwhile 'dining at seven . . . going to bed at three and lying in bed till four. She has hysterical fits in a morning and dances in the evening; she bathes, rides, dances for ten days and lies in bed the next ten'. So reported Lady Sarah Lennox. Selina, up in her nursery fortress was quietly enlivening the children's lessons by use of the magic lantern just as Madame de Genlis in France was using one to teach history to her pupils. Earlier, Horace Walpole had written to a friend that the Duchess's passion for gambling was so reckless that she might forget her good resolution about nursing her child. It was certainly as well that her little daughters had the security of Selina's guardianship but Georgiana had her children's welfare close to her heart, nevertheless. She was in constant touch with their governess about their education and well-being and saw to it that they learnt more useful things than the elegant accomplishments so popular at the time, even if she was away in France for Harriet's fourth birthday.

The days passed uneventfully at Chatsworth where Selina had a room of her own, even if it was up in the roof overlooking the courtyard with only a view of the back of the busts which later on were taken down to decorate the greenhouse. Luckily Selina's temperament was as calm as her mother's and she must have been a godsend to that higgledy-piggledy collection of children, particularly when Caro Ponsonby was giving an exhibition of her celebrated tantrums. Nor was it all work and no play, as there were charades and concerts at home as well as going to the Opera and visits to the seaside. One holiday at Ramsgate was not much appreciated. There was nothing to do but go long walks to the pier under a scorching sun or along the cliffs with a sedate dip in the sea, which was all they really looked forward to, fettered though they were by all-enveloping bathing suits under Selina's watchful care.

By this time the little governess had become so much one of the family, talking about *her* dear children, that when a suggestion from the Prince of Wales came that she should change her situation to the more exalted post of 'sub-preceptress' to Princess Charlotte, she declined this honour. It is unlikely that she would have found any more pleasure in Court circles than Fanny Burney did when she unwisely gave in to her father's and elderly friend Mrs Delany's wishes by accepting the uncomfortable post of Keeper of the Robes under the detestable Mrs Schwellenbergen. The household of the Prince Regent and that of his eccentric wife Princess Caroline, together with all the interference and quarrels stemming from their incompatability, not to mention Queen Charlotte and King George's interventions, would have been a poor exchange for the cosy little eyrie at Chatsworth and the lively, unconventional household of the Duchess of Devonshire.

Then in 1806 the vital, warm-hearted Duchess died after a painfully drawn-out illness. Lady Elizabeth Foster took command at Devonshire House with Selina, who was recalled from Chatsworth, as a chaperone. This arrangement doesn't sound very easy nor very gay. The eldest Cavendish daughter, Hary-o, was constantly bickering with Lady Elizabeth and all poor Selina could think of doing was to talk on some religious subject. She had never liked Lady Elizabeth and as for the future second Duchess, she compared the governess with the north east wind which 'in the brightest sunshine still has some chill in it'. Now the wily old Dowager Duchess, who first put Selina in her position, stepped in as peacemaker. Hary-o was devoted to her moralising strait-laced governess and called her 'my best and dearest friend'. Selina remained a rock on which all her 'dear children' leant in times of trouble. She read the confidential letters they wrote to her as they grew up to tell her about their love-affairs. She was the best type of confidant as she never gossiped nor discussed their affairs. The very fact that she was so prim and rigid in her standards made her the most secure of friends for the children to rely upon. Whatever high principles of stableness of character any of them may have had must have come from Selina's example.

First her own mother died and then old Lady Spencer. The children began to have children of their own and still Selina lived on in the little room referred to as the 'Upper Bow', peopling it with her memories and being visited by her pupils until she died at the beginning of January 1829.

MARIA EDGEWORTH
1767–1849

Richard Edgeworth was a fellow of the Royal Society. He was a most distinguished man, numbering amongst his many accomplishments a good working knowledge of engineering and chemistry, as well as a sound basis of moral philosophy. He was born at Bath in 1744. Certainly he must have been uxorious since, believe it or not, he had no less than four wives and 21 children. Maria was the second of three children from his first marriage to Anna-Maria Elers. This, as it happened, was his only unhappy venture into matrimony. She died in 1773 when she was only twenty. Her husband instantly married Honora Sneyd, who died seven years later, when he once more married immediately, Elizabeth Sneyd. She lived with him happily for seventeen years until 1797 and finally, the year after her death he married his last wife, Frances Anne Beaufort, who died in 1865, outliving both her husband and her famous stepdaughter, Maria Edgeworth.

When Maria was fifteen she set forth with her father, stepmother and brothers and sisters for Edgeworthstown, where her father decided he had a duty towards his Irish estates. There she lived for the rest of her life.

Maria was only 4 feet and 7 inches when she was grown up and had never been pretty. However, what she lacked in stature and beauty she made up for in brains. After she had spent nine miserable months in a fashionable boarding school in Wimpole Street, her father brought her home and it was his love and admiration that turned the ugly duckling into a self-confident swan of great learning and accomplishments. It was therefore not surprising that she was devoted to her papa. Although she was never a governess, in the true sense of the word, since she was not paid for her services in the family, of course, nevertheless she must, for the purposes of this book, qualify as a teacher. She educated her little brothers and sisters, and in collaboration with her brilliant father, she formed a theory of education and put it into practice, subsequently writing an enormous number of excellent books that are forgotten now, but really could be classified as minor classics. If, therefore, we define governess as it is expressed in the *Oxford Dictionary*, 'female teacher, especially of children, in a private household', Maria most certainly comes under our heading to this chapter on governesses.

In fact, one of her books was called *The Good Governess, (Moral Tales)*. This described a heroine taking her charges to a toy shop that might well be one of those we visit in this year of grace 1973, instead of almost 200 years ago. One child chose a small loom for weaving ribbons, another asked to have materials for making baskets. The boy selected a printing press and some gardening tools. 'Rational toys for the rising generation', was how Maria described them.

The Edgeworth children were always surrounded by older members of their family, but were never allowed to mix with the servants, to their loss, one would have thought. The library was given over to the children and here they were taught, here they played. Oddly enough, there was a lack of religious teaching; though perhaps not so odd when we remember that Maria and her father's educational theories were based on Rousseau and Madame de Genlis.*

In 1798 father and daughter published a work called *Practical Education*. This was basically a description of how the young Edgeworths were brought up. It was not, as it happened, plain sailing. Richard Edgeworth found that Rousseau's principles did not work with his eldest son. The boy was completely wild and ungovernable and when he died at an early age his father was uncompromisingly frank about it. He observed drily, 'It is better he has retired from the scene'. Perhaps it would have been better still if he had not been brought up on Rousseau's educational theories. 'Rousseau', said Dr Johnson, 'is a very bad man'. 'Sir, do you think him as bad a man as Voltaire?' asked Boswell. 'Why, Sir,' replied Johnson, 'it is difficult to settle the proportion of iniquity between them'. Rousseau's treatise on education advocated a return to nature and instruction based on the observation of natural phenomena.

Practical Education was strongly criticised by many readers, particularly as there was no religious teaching in it. However, as the children were taken to church regularly and taught to read the Bible, it seems that this was rather better than stuffing them with the exceedingly gloomy religion that the little Fairchilds, for instance, had to endure; all hell-fire and original sin. The Edgeworth theme was, 'we all try, and we ought to try, to make ourselves as happy as we can, without hurting anybody else'. What is the matter with that, I wonder?

*Madame de Genlis (1746–1830) lived in Paris from 1758. She married in 1762 and after her unlucky husband was beheaded by the Revolutionaries in 1793, she emigrated, and only returned to France in 1802. She lived by her pen from 1793 till 1802 in Switzerland and England writing prolifically, mostly novels. She became a governess to the children of the Duchesse de Chartres, one of them being Louis-Philippe. She too was interested in the so-called 'practical' education.

Maria followed up their joint book on *Practical Education* with a work published under her own name called *Early Lessons*. This was intended to be a supplement to *Practical Education*, and it was written in what was then the popular form of 'questions and answers'. The little hero Frank learns such useful lessons as how to make rush candles and how to brew beer, and his sister Rosamund is taught by her almost pathologically rational mother the consequences of choosing pretty rather than useful presents. Both parents were strong believers that reason always conquers the irrational.

Maria's books were memorable for their excellent presentation of the life of children in a lively and interesting way. Moral they were, of course, but then many children's books continue to be so to this day. Where Maria succeeded was on the entertainment side. Her tales were well written, full of good character drawing and they were meant to amuse the young readers and not only to instruct them. The Edgeworths system of education, however, never really became generally accepted until its principles were revived in the 1930s.

One of Maria's stories has remained in my mind from the days when my grandmother read it to me in the First World War. It was called *Waste Not, Want Not* and told the vivid and even witty story of the poor boy Ben who was able in his turn to help his patron, which was a typically Georgian theme. The setting, by the way, is fashionable Bath. The rich boy had heedlessly cut the knots of a string round his parcel, whilst poor Ben saved his own carefully for some future possible use. As luck would have it the rich boy was taking part in an archery competition and broke the cord on his bow. So poor Ben was able proudly to step forward and save the day. He offered his string, so wisely saved, to mend the bow and win the match.

The Edgeworth method was more humane in some respects than the eighteenth century flogging and rule of fear which was more general; but there is something rather chill and heartless in this cool system of reasoning and argument. Instant obedience was the keynote of most nurseries both in Georgian and Victorian days. The only difference was that obedience was a religious duty to the Victorians and just part of the established order of life for the Georgians. Mrs Sherwood, the fourth part of whose book *The Fairchild Family** was published as late as 1847, chose the best of both worlds and advised chastisement as the first punishment,

*The first part appeared in 1818.

followed by ostracism, if flogging failed. This combination of Georgian savagery and Victorian mental cruelty was terrible indeed. The wonder is that most of the nation did not develop into raging psychiatric maniacs. It was, of course, an Age of violence. The end of the eighteenth century saw Europe torn apart by the French Revolution, and Prinny certainly did nothing to put royalty back into repute. The complacency of the upper classes was over; political disorder, instability and scandal reigned. Then came the defeat of Napoleon in 1815 and the pendulum began to swing towards economic recovery and empire-building with a restoration of the national prestige.

Though so many people were living through all these disturbances with hardly a ripple breaking over their quiet lives, the discipline in the nurseries and schoolrooms was perhaps a subconscious attempt to find an antidote to the disorder and instability in the world. Parents were always anxious to instil the virtues of obedience, charity towards the poor and religion into their children and as most of the governesses and some of the writers for children came from families connected with the clergy this was easily provided. Mrs Trimmer was much interested in Sunday Schools for the poor. Her Charity School Spelling Books had improving little stories in them in the usual high moral tone. The Brontës, all of whom were teaching as governesses at some time, were the daughters of a clergyman. Mrs Gatty was a clergyman's wife and both she and her daughter Juliana Horatia Ewing wrote for children. Mrs Sherwood was the daughter of a clergyman too. It was, however, in the nineteenth century that the religious child came into its own. The eighteenth century child was expected to be diligent and punctual rather than pious. The religious tracts appeared in the nineteenth century. *The Tale of Warning, or the Victims of Indolence* is the kind of title we find in 1810, and the story is invariably that in which the bad child is contrasted unfavourably with the good one, virtue always being satisfactorily rewarded. Why not? We still enjoy the wild west cowboy stories when the hero is guaranteed to come through triumphant whilst the baddies are discomfited. These books were of course a great help to governesses as well as parents, even though few of them, apart from Maria Edgeworth's stories, had much literary merit.

ELLEN WEETON
1776–c. 1844

One aspect of being a governess was the sense of inferiority it seems to have given these intelligent and gifted, but poverty-stricken ladies. Selina Trimmer in her happy position with the Devonshires was never allowed to feel inferior. On the contrary, she was loved and respected and consulted by all the family and she blossomed in this happy atmosphere. True, there were never opportunities for marriage, even though her pupils used to tease her at one time about a Mr Adair, who was a frequent visitor to Devonshire House. Most governesses, at one time or another, must have wished they were bringing up their own children instead of other people's. Poor Ellen* Weeton was so cowed by her poverty and the singularly unfortunate life she led, that when she fell in love with a most suitable clergyman called Mr Saul, who came to stay with one of her employers, she was so eaten up with a sense of her own unworthiness that she wrote, 'the great difference between a governess and clergyman of family and fortune made me cautious of being in his company more than I could help, lest my heart should be involuntarily forming an attachment that might cause me years of unhappiness'. Unfortunately her heart had already formed its attachment, and eventually all the poor girl could do was to give up her job and find another one. Her tall, unprepossessing appearance was not calculated to stir romantic yearnings in the male breast, but at least she was more than usually clever. Alas, this seems to have exacerbated her troubles, for she laboured under a cruel sense of the unfairness of a world where her stupid young brother was given all the education he was incapable of appreciating, whilst she had to slave in order to get him into the legal profession. It is very sad to read her journals, full of constant setbacks and misfortunes, but even sadder to realise how indifferent people are to the sufferings of others, more particularly when those others are unattractive girls with neither the magnetism of charm, beauty nor a sense of humour. Of course, we none of us have much sense of humour left when all goes wrong and nothing goes right, if it comes to that.

In Ellen's case her trouble was that she had to find her jobs in the rising, disdainful middle classes, just as the Brontës had to do later. They none of them had the luck of being placed in aristocratic homes, where their position would have been quite different. We have already seen that in the eighteenth century, at least, it was considered exceedingly ill-bred to treat the governess or tutor with contempt. *Jane Eyre's* 'the Honourable Blanche Ingram', with her ill-natured asides about them, does not ring quite true;

*'. . . next myself, born of Christmas Day, 1776 and christened by the name of Nelly'. But she preferred Ellen.
†Exact date unknown.

94

but then Charlotte Brontë probably never met anyone like the Devonshire House set.

Ellen Weeton had another unusual cross to bear. Her father had been the captain of a slave-ship. True, he had died when she was only five, but 1807 saw the abolition of the slave trade. Long before that, when Ellen was a girl, there was a trend towards humanitarianism and philanthropy, which would not have recommended the daughter of a slave-ship captain to her middle class employers. Perhaps she kept it a secret, but it would not have helped her self-esteem.

From childhood, Ellen had been a glutton for knowledge. She confessed that she 'burned to learn Latin, French, the Arts, the Sciences'. Instead she was tied to helping her mother to run a little dame's school, working there for as many as nine hours a day and then, instead of studying her beloved books, she had to help with all the chores of cooking, sewing and housework. On top of everything else, her poor mother suffered from asthma, a psychosomatic disease, for which we can easily understand the reason.

At least Ellen had the satisfaction of getting young Tom, her brother, apprenticed to a solicitor, but another disaster faced her when she was twenty-one. Her unfortunate mother died and, struggle on as she could, there came a time when she had to give up the school and try to get herself a post as a governess. All this time her food had been barely at subsistence level, so she was, into the bargain, not at all well. Tom did his best to try to help his sister find work but it came to nothing and finally she took a thoroughly uncongenial job as a guest-companion. This, predictably, did not last long, and presently her one girl-friend, Ann Winkley, who lived in Liverpool, took her in as a lodger.

Probably her most soul-destroying experience was when she applied for and got a job in Ambleside, at the princely sum of 30 guineas a year. The house had the attractive name of Dove's Nest and it stood in the pleasant setting of a park sloping down to Windermere. All was delightful except for the child she was to look after. Her employer, Mr Pedder, had married *en secondes noces* a girl of seventeen, and the child, a girl of ten, was his daughter by a previous marriage. It had to happen to Ellen Weeton. Yes, the girl was subject to fits. Moreover, Ellen had to cope with these distressing occurrences, sometimes four or five times a day. She told the whole dreadful story to Ann Winkley; but even worse was to come. One day, the little girl stood too near an open fire and set her clothes alight. Ellen behaved with commendable courage and swiftness, but a few hours later the child was dead.

95

Without much alternative the unhappy Ellen stayed on as companion to the young wife, but what with Mr Saul the fascinating clergyman's visits and then Mr Pedder, her employer, in a constant state of inebriation, Ellen had to move once more. As it happened she later on met a far less attractive person than Mr Saul and alas, she married him. We can picture her useful and busy life as a clergyman's wife; but the picture is a mirage, as we shall see.

Her next employment was looking after an unruly band of little Armitages, near Huddersfield. From seven in the morning until seven or eight at night Ellen was in charge of the children, whom she describes as 'noisy, insolent, quarrelsome and ill-tempered'.

Mr Armitage was a successful industrialist, but he was not in the least interested in his children's education, nor was he ready to spend sixpence on books or other amenities for the schoolroom; though he did finally give in to Ellen's persistent demands. The Armitages were only keeping up with the Joneses in having a governess. With the emergence of what the eighteenth century called 'the middling sort', architects and apothecaries became respectable and there were more opportunities for 'betterment'. The satirists, both in word and pictures, found a bottomless pit of amusement picking out the pretensions and vulgarities of the *nouveau riche*. There were more levels of 'upper middle' and 'lower middle' than before, and social ambitions were consequently rife. The landed gentry looked on with distaste, but were quite prepared to let their sons and daughters marry these 'middling sort' provided the money was right.

Ellen was, quite happy at the Armitages until she found that Mrs Armitage was in a state of continual pregnancy, and the thought of more and more little dears in the nursery made her quail. Nobody seems to have wanted her to leave. They called her affectionately their dear Ugly-face, but go she did, and in fact she never took up another position as governess after this.

It is a curious fact that some unlucky people seem to have been singled out by the fates for misfortune. Whether this is partly their own fault, on the principle of the old cliché, 'think lucky and you'll be lucky' and they always expect to be dogged by disasters; or whether it simply *is* bad luck, who can say? Ellen certainly does not seem to have had any chance at all. She subsequently met a villain called Aaron Stock and was foolish enough to marry him. She and her daughter Mary were utterly miserable and ill-treated. If only she could have known that one day she would be famous through her journals and letters, how happy that would have made

her. Let us hope that her poor, sad spirit somehow has found rest
in this knowledge.

THE BRONTËS
CHARLOTTE (1816–55) EMILY (1818–48)
ANNE (1820–49)

Probably the best known governesses of all time are the three
talented Brontë girls. Emily had more than talent; she was a genius.
Charlotte was unusually gifted, and the third sister, gentle and
pious Anne, was also a considerable writer. The difference between
them was that where Emily wrote outside herself, the other two
used their experiences as a base on which to build their novels.
Thanks to Charlotte their books were published under pseudonyms.
But before this they all went out teaching.

Charlotte wrote in 1848, 'A governess's experience is frequently
indeed bitter, but its results are precious'. The results sound
depressingly austere. An improved character through 'painful
but priceless' discipline of the mind could surely have been bought
at a lower price than the long months of servitude she endured,
denying herself even the pleasures of reading and writing except
in her rare moments of leisure. But Charlotte was a pioneer in the
sphere of independence for women. She was determined she and
her sisters should carve out careers as teachers.

The Sidgwick's household was her first private post and her
silent vigils in their drawing-room, ignored and despised, were
afterwards transformed into Jane Eyre's experiences with the
'Honourable Blanche Ingram', the ill-mannered daughter of Lord
Ingram. The Sidgwicks requested her to walk to church 'a little
behind them'. How Charlotte's proud soul must have been seared
by such incredibly small-minded behaviour. Alas, she had no sense
of humour to buttress her against this sort of treatment. Jane
Austen, like her own heroine Elizabeth Bennett, would have laughed
merrily to herself and written a sharp, witty account to her sister.
Not surprisingly, Charlotte became ill due to all the tensions and
stress she endured, and her next post was not taken until eight
months after she left the Sidgwicks.

The Whites of Rawdon near Bradford, where she went next,
were unashamedly *nouveaux riches,* and on the whole were pleasantly
respectful of Charlotte's talents and the fact that she was a clergyman's daughter. She was convinced that the White's 'extraction
is very low'; Mrs White was an exciseman's daughter. Although
this post was far more congenial than the Sidgwick's household of

Emily Brontë, painted by her brother Branwell, when she was 15.
Courtesy of the National Portrait Gallery.

'riotous little fiends', Charlotte only stayed here for six months, leaving with regrets on both sides. She had liked Mr White very much and grew to find that Mrs White was 'a good sort of body in spite of all her bouncing and boasting, her bad grammar and worse orthography'. She even sent a gift to the little Sarah White, a book which she inscribed and dated 20 July 1841.

Six years later *Jane Eyre* was published, receiving immediate recognition and admiration. Her success she considered was the direct result of her hard-worked, ill-paid and largely unrewarding career as a governess. Still, she was able to recommend the life to a friend's daughter as being preferable to staying at home and doing nothing. This may seem faint praise, but with her lack of vitality, her shyness among strangers, her quiet ways and reserved manner, Charlotte was not really equipped for ruling a family of rampageous children.

Emily Brontë was even less suited to the life of a teacher. She went nevertheless to Miss Patchett's Academy for Young Ladies, a gaunt house set in savage moorland scenery near Halifax. In 1838 Emily was pouring out her feelings in poetry and describing the 'walls of my dark prison house'. Her wild, strange spirit was too strong to be battered by her experiences as a governess and she, like Charlotte, made use of this self-imposed penance by transforming it into that marvellous, haunting, magical story of *Wuthering Heights*. Her fierce independence under the yoke of Miss Patchett's harsh régime was apparently untouched by this experience and in fact her genius seems to have blossomed in adversity. She preferred the austere to the pampered life and she benefited from the flowerless, desolate moors near Halifax just as she found inspiration in the Haworth scenery where 'damp stands in the long green grass, as thick as morning's tears', when she returned home to the 'blue mists, sweet mists' of the moors she knew and loved so well. Emily was unique. It is impossible to imagine her fettered to a schoolroom and the reports that she was 'not unpopular' with her pupils sound so negative a state as to suggest that both she and her pupils were mutually indifferent to each other's company. What she managed to teach them we shall never know. There are no memories which have been handed down like the gift of the book from Charlotte to a favourite pupil. Emily, like Charlotte, pined for home and so she in turn had to give up trying to earn a living and to help pay her wastrel brother Branwell's debts. Nevertheless she did join Charlotte for a time in Brussels to learn French. That subject was one they all lacked and all felt the lack of since languages were always asked for in 'the best households'.

99

H

The last of the sisters to become a governess was the least forceful personality, Anne. She set off from their remote but dearly loved home to seek her fortune at the age of nineteen. It was on a wintry March day in 1839 that she started out to chart unknown waters at Mrs Ingham's house, Blake Hall. In her turn the experience was minted by imagination into a novel, *Agnes Grey*. Gentle, dear Anne, who in reply to her father's question to her at the age of four, 'What does a child like you want most?' answered, 'Age and experience!' Well, she was getting it now. Her stay at Blake Hall lasted until her first holiday the following Christmas and after that she decided to try her luck elsewhere. Like her sisters Anne, too, was not possessed of that saving grace the ability to laugh at her situation, though she was less touchy than Charlotte over slights. She was gentler, with a sweeter nature than either of her brilliant sisters and she made such friends with the next girls she taught that they kept in touch with her for the rest of her life.

Her new situation was an environment she knew how to tackle, a clergyman's household. The Robinsons were kind, the two girls congenial and the little parish in the valley of river, water-meadows and gracious trees, was a complete contrast to the bleak, grey stone cottages and windswept moorlands round Haworth Parsonage. Anne wrote about her life as a governess quietly, factually but vividly. She had long periods of loneliness and home-sickness, but her nature was to accept rather than to fight back.

Into this tranquil household of the Robinsons disruption came in the shape of the sisters' dissolute unhappy brother Branwell who joined her as a tutor. Soon he was causing considerable havoc in the calm early Victorian household, having dreamed himself into an overpowering passion for Mrs Robinson, which was not assuaged by his resorts to the local inn for consolation. Anne was obliged to leave the Robinsons, despite their protests. Home she went, even perhaps forgiving Branwell in her heart for his drunkenness and his opium-eating, as it brought her back to the home they all so much hated to leave.

In 1845 she wrote, 'I have had some very unpleasant and undreamt of experience of human nature', and she embarked on *The Tenant of Wildfell Hall* as a horrible warning. A melancholy little preface appeared in the second edition, written by the author, in which Acton Bell admits, 'I knew that such characters (as Huntingdon and his cronies) do exist, and if I have warned one rash youth from following in their step, the book has not been written in vain'.

Her first book, *Agnes Grey*, was written late in 1845 whilst her two sisters were composing *The Professor* and *Wuthering Heights*.

As it happened, *Jane Eyre*, written in 1846, was the first Brontë novel to appear. After searching for a publisher for eighteen months Charlotte found Smith Elder and Co., who took the wise and profitable step of launching the books by Currer, Ellis and Acton Bell. The rest of the story does not concern us here, but the magic of the Brontës' story has never since dimmed. The three obscure governesses of Haworth are immortal.

★★★★★

By way of a footnote to this chapter about a few selected from the army of governesses who have quietly brought up some of the children of England for so many centuries; an antique-shop recently yielded a little bonus in the shape of a '*Times*' newspaper dated Monday, January 19, 1807. The format is little changed from what it was up to a few years ago, when advertisements were on the front page. In the third column the following announcement appeared:

'GOVERNESS.—WANTS a SITUATION as GOVERNESS, a young Lady who will undertake to teach the English, French and Italian languages, grammatically; also Geography; she can likewise give instruction on the Harp and Pianoforte. The most unexceptional references can be produced with regard to family and qualifications. Address post paid to Miss T. at Mr Poole's Juvenile Library, Pall Mall'.

There speaks the voice of the Georgian governess across the years. Today hardly any of the profession remain, and except in so far as she blazed the way for our brave new world of education for everyone, we cannot regret her departure.

CHAPTER SIX

Literary Children

In Chapter Two we met prodigies or exceptional children who have been remembered for outstanding early abilities. They sometimes, but not always, developed into equally exceptional adults. Here we shall be meeting children influenced by literature. Two of our subjects wrote later in life for children. The other three kept journals or diaries in childhood. The first of these, Fanny Burney, subsequently became a celebrated novelist. These children were not prodigies, but they represent the borderline between the infant prodigy who made good and the gifted child who developed at an average pace to become a writer or to be associated with literary giants, as happened to Queeney Thrale. The nineteenth century saw the final flowering of letter-writers and diarists. Their very triviality is of value to us today in illuminating a way of life that has long departed, starting perhaps, in the seventeenth century when Sir William Dugdale kept his diary for about forty-five years, from the age of thirty-seven when he began it. The diaries of children are much rarer, of course, though probably many more wrote them and tore them up later.

A little Scottish girl called Flora Moir was born in 1839 at 41 Charlotte Square, Edinburgh and lived there all her childhood. When she was married in the 1860s she decided to write her memoirs of childhood for the amusement of her own offspring. She recalled a gay wedding in the Square, with all the carriages arriving and the servants resplendent in liveries of light blue and crimson. One of her first nurses was called Mary Markwich, and later on Flora was told that the girl was a workhouse foundling called after the place where she was deserted. Flora charitably remarks that 'she must have been a very respectable, steady girl to have worked her way up from such a beginning, but her workhouse training made her awfully harsh and unkind'. She rubbed the soap into her charge's eyes and mouth when she washed her and shook the child and pushed her into a cupboard when she screamed out in protest. It is a melancholy reminder of what workhouse children must have been subjected to themselves, with no parents to come to the rescue and dismiss the tyrant, until Dickens took up their cause.

Going to church brought painful memories to Flora. She had been afraid that the clergyman would 'fly out of the pulpit upon us just below'. Earlier, aged three, she was carried howling out of church because the minister 'preached too hard'. Flora's recollections included toys like jigsaw puzzles and tin soldiers and a large battered doll with blue kid arms, suggesting her vintage to have been about 1840, whom Flora christened 'Enormity'. Papa once brought back a bonbon box in the form of a bear sitting on his hind legs. When his head was removed behold he was stuffed with lovely sweets in imitation of fruits. There was a farmyard toy and a box of 'Mr Urquhart's bricks'. These old toys were all given away to deserving children so that she had nothing left to pass on to her own.

As late as the 1840s people in Edinburgh were taking sedan-chairs to their destinations and the two chief 'caddies' at Charlotte Square were quite ready to carry four children at a time. At this period it was customary to go to church in a sedan-chair if the weather was bad and the pavements would be crowded with a continuous stream of people and several sedan-chairs. Cabs were considered wrong because they prevented the driver from getting to church, but the sedan-chair could stand in the vestibule whilst the 'caddies' came into the service. At least, that was the idea.

The postman used to wear a scarlet tail coat and a shiny 'topper' with a smart cockade, and many other passages in Flora's memoirs recall customs which have long since been forgotten. However, the journal about childhood written in maturity is never quite as convincing as the child's own words. Our first writer was an eighteenth century child, born in 1752.

FANNY BURNEY
1752–1840

Fanny's mother was the grand-daughter of a Huguenot and therefore French was as much her language as English. She even translated Maupertuis and was 'reading the best authors' at every opportunity. Fanny herself was very slow in learning to read and her sister Susan, who was three years younger, could read before Fanny had mastered the alphabet. She wrote to Susan, 'I recollect you spouting passages from Pope that I learned from hearing you recite them'. Her dullness was clearly of no great consequence and her mother was certainly never deceived by it, even though others might call the child 'the little dunce'. Those nearest to her always thought of her as wise, considerate and thoughtful. She inherited her diffidence from her father Dr Burney who managed to conceal his shyness behind polished manners whereas Fanny never conquered hers. 'Nobody, I believe, has so *very* little command of countenance as myself', she wrote later. 'I could feel my whole face on fire'. Like many people who are shy Fanny was an extremely good letter writer and kept her journal from the age of 16, beginning to write it in 1768. She had written many attempts at novels and even plays before this but was persuaded to burn the lot.

Poor Fanny lost her mother in 1761 when she was only nine and a friend noticing her agony of grief said she had 'never met with a child of such intense and acute feelings'. Dr Burney was equally afflicted and perhaps this mutual distress drew them together into a particularly close relationship. He had five other children. Luckily Dr Burney married again in 1767 most happily and Fanny never spoke anything but praise of her step-mother Elizabeth Allen. This argues considerable tact on the part of the new Mrs Burney. She herself had two children by Dr Burney, Richard Thomas and Sarah Harriet who later became a novelist. By her first husband she had three children. Elizabeth Allen was described by Dr Burney as being of 'a cultivated mind, intellects above the general level of her sex and with a curiosity after knowledge insatiable to the last'. She must have been a kind warm personality and she certainly adored her second husband. It was a love-match and not 'arranged' as her first marriage to a cousin had been. She set great value on Fanny's head and heart.

It must be rare that a girl of just sixteen, writing her diary, should foresee the pleasure she would get in her old age from re-reading it. Fanny had a warm heart and a warm-hearted family who even in her backward childhood recognised her remarkable gifts of mind, memory and mimicry.

'Our most beloved Mr Crisp' was a self-appointed adopted father of the young Burneys and took an especial interest in Fanny's journals. Indeed they and her letters were the chief pleasure of his old age. He had been a patron of Dr Burney and became a life-long friend though 20 years his senior. He was a man of fashion, culture and wit, a friend of such men as Johnson, Neville, Garrick and other men of letters as well as being a welcome guest of the Duchess of Portland and Mrs Delany and an acquaintance with Mrs Montagu, the Bluestocking, of whom he wrote later to Fanny 'in my own private mind's pocket book I set her down for a vain empty, conceited pretender and little else'.

Fanny must have been wiry like her father, as she lived to the ripe old age of eighty-nine, but she was small and subject to very bad coughs and colds. Her mother had died of consumption which was a common disease in the eighteenth century. She had wit and charm for those whom she allowed to get to know her, but shyness dogged her all her life.

The Burneys had left Kings Lynn in 1760 for London, where Dr Burney became one of the most sought-after music-masters of his day, as well as composing music and compiling his great *chef d'oeuvre* on the History of Music. The family lived in Poland Street in London next to a wig-maker's shop and near a friend called Mrs Pringle, who was always ready to welcome and make much of Fanny and her sister Hetty. The children's 'playroom' was nothing more than a closet at the top of two flights of stairs where the younger ones kept all their toys. We long to know what toys they had— possibly one of those delightful wooden dolls with painted faces, inset black glass eyes and spoon shaped hands, dressed in the fashionable silk dresses of the day and wearing a tall wig. Here Fanny wrote her first plays and novels which alas she burnt on a funeral pyre on the paved court below when she was fifteen.

There were three 'parlours' in the house and commodes stood in the dining-room cheek by jowl with Mrs Burney's bureau. Perhaps this was one better than the customary pewter or silver chamber-pot usually kept in the cupboard of the sideboard. These, as well as the early nineteenth century china ones are collector's pieces today. Dr Burney's bureau was also there and in it he kept not only his private papers but the money he earned in fees. Once a former footman of theirs, who knew the ways of the household only too well, broke in and robbed the doctor of £300.

It is interesting to anyone with a taste for the small change of history to find that much later in 1777 Fanny wrote, 'chocolate being brought we adjoined to the dining-room'. When, as Madame d'Arblay, she edited her early diary the word is changed to 'drawing-room'. She did not in fact say 'drawing-room' until she had been to Court. In her Windsor diary she writes 'the *drawing-room* as they call it *here*'. That arbiter of correct behaviour Mrs Delany speaks in 1755 of her '*dining-room*, vulgarly so called'. In fact the old words in most common use were *parlour* for any sitting-room, eating or dining parlour and for rooms distinct from those used for reception, *chamber* or *bed-chamber*.

Returning to Poland Street we hear that a Mr Boone broke his sword clambering up the steep stairs and thanked his stars he had not broken his neck. However, his host remarked blandly,

'That speaks ill for my stairs—but they were constructed by *Sir Isaac Newton* not by *me*.' We therefore may assume that the illustrious mathematician, physicist, astronomer and philosopher built the house. He died in 1727.

Sometimes Aunt Ann would drop in from her house in York Street, to have tea with the family, sincerely praying she would not be obliged to meet any of the 'foreigners' who so often called on the Doctor. Piozzi, the violinist who became Mrs Thrale's second husband often came, touchy and jealous, according to Fanny's sister Susan. Baretti and Merlin, Pacchierotti, the castrato singer of whom they were all so fond, and Mr Penneck of the British Museum could be expected to be guests of the Burneys; and so could Dr Johnson, perhaps bringing his blind friend Mrs Williams from St Martin's Street. Uninvited guests seem to have usually left the house by 11 o'clock in the evening and this gave the family time for supper and, as Fanny put it, 'an excuse for chatting over baked apples'.

Mrs Burney often went to see her mother and others of her family at Lynn and sometimes Fanny and Susan also went for a change of air. Dr Burney at home was busy giving music lessons from seven or eight in the morning until late in the afternoon and after that he would be writing in his study.

In July 1768 Fanny is at Lynn and lets out a little *cri-de-coeur* about the 'tittle tattle, prittle prattle visitants'. 'Oh dear', she writes, 'I am so tired of . . . these fall lall people!' In short, she considers that in a country town all their conversation is scandal and all their attention is on dress, 'folly, envy and censoriousness'. She decides a city or a village are the only places to be comfortable in, for 'a Country Town I think has all the bad qualities without one of the good ones of both'. That is her summing-up of the situation at the age of sixteen.

Here at Lynn Regis* they breakfasted at ten, having risen from bed as early as they liked. They dined at two, drank tea about six and supped at nine. Fanny wisely disciplined herself into joining in activities with the rest of the party or occupying herself with needlework in the morning, indulging herself in her 'two *most* favourite pursuits, reading and writing', in the afternoons.

One morning in July she had the excitement of seeing 'a *publick* Wedding'. The affair had long been 'in agitation' due to the inferiority of the bridegroom's fortune. However, the match eventually was decided upon and from their house 'in the churchyard exactly

*King's Lynn today.

opposite the great church door. the Burneys had an excellent view of the procession and the 'prodidgious' (sic) mob that was in attendance. Fanny at sixteen was no starry-eyed romantic. She remarked 'O how short a time does it take to put an eternal end to a woman's liberty!' She added, 'I don't think they were a quarter of an hour in the Church altogether. Lord bless me! it would not be time enough, I should think, for a poor creature to see where she was'. 'However, the church bells rang merrily and loud and the doors opened and we saw them walk down the Isle', (sic) reported Fanny. The bridegroom looked suitably gay and happy and apparently equally suitable was the bride's grave but not sad face. Fanny ended her entry in the journal, 'I don't suppose any thing can be so dreadful as a publick wedding—my stars! I should never be able to support it! . . . '. At breakfast they had a long conversation on matrimony. Presumably the wedding took place before 10 o'clock and the guests joined in a wedding breakfast which we now would celebrate at midday or later.

The byways of history bring us many unexpected little bonuses. Fanny's friend Mrs Thrale, born in 1741 and thus eleven years older than herself, wrote in her *Thraliana*, a sort of commonplace book which she insisted was not ever intended for publication, 'Yesterday I dined at Sir Joshua Reynolds, Richmond Hill, some agreeable people were raked together and we intended to have a charming day of it. But Mr Garrick was sick and Lady Rothes was troublesome. She brought the Babies with her, both under six years old, which though the prettiest Babies in the World were not wanted there at all. They played and prattled and suffered nobody to be heard but themselves, we ancient maids, sterile wives and disappointed parents were peevish to see others happier than ourselves in a little Boy, who, naughty as we called him, three people there would have been glad to purchase with 10,000 pounds —Garrick, Thrale and old Deputy Paterson, who married a second wife on purpose but could not obtain his wish'.

So even Lady Rothes in those days took her children to grown-up parties. Was it to show them off, as Jane Austen's Lady Middleton in *Sense and Sensibility* always did with her spoilt little Henry? They all had nurses or governesses to look after them. The Duchess of Devonshire certainly kept her brood out of sight at receptions and parties, under the wing of Selina Trimmer, whom we have already met. Yet looking at pictures of the eighteenth and even early nineteenth century we frequently find 'the darling young' joining in walks in the park or visits to the seaside, even watching cricket matches or having tea in the drawing-room with their upper-class parents. Perhaps generally speaking they were not banished to their nurseries so much until the nineteenth century.

Mrs Thrale is often accused of indifference, not to say dislike of her children. Yet she wrote in *Thraliana*, 'I catch myself thinking that if my Master was to dye, and Queeny to marry; I would take my next two Girls and give them a little Run upon the Continent before the time of flirtation should arrive, as School Girls are dangerous animals, enough at 14 or 15 years old. Ignorant of every earthly thing but their Lessons, they are a natural Prey to all who venture the Attack . . .'. It is of course possible that in spite of her protestations to the contrary she did hope *Thraliana* would eventually be published.

Fanny's diaries are remarkable for their author's imagination, charm and natural ability to express herself. In fact she was a born writer and she never stopped those entries in her diaries from the age of sixteen to the last sentences she wrote in March 1839 when she was eighty-nine. But as we read them one important fact emerges, and this is her obvious preference for her older friends. Due to her dependence and deep affection for her father she seems to have surrounded herself with devoted admirers like Mr Samuel Crisp of Chessington, for whom she wrote her early journals, and Dr Johnson whom she loved dearly also. Mrs Thrale was eleven years older as we have seen, and Fanny was devoted to her. She referred to parsimonious, disagreeable old Charlotte as the 'sweet Queen'. Even though, when at Court, she fled terrified from the mad old King, she was very fond of him too and fond also of Mrs Delany, who really must have been not only unbearably snobbish but also a bit of a bore. Fanny's witty and amusing novels show *she* certainly was not a bore, however. Both Fanny and Susan were also smitten with the charms of David Garrick, a frequent visitor to Dr Burney's house. As he was born in 1717 this famous actor was no spring chicken at the time when Fanny was writing her diaries at sixteen years old. He was in fact 35 years her senior. However, he was gay and witty and always welcome in Poland Street. Another *vignette* of the period comes from Fanny. In 1775 she reported that Garrick asked her father, 'When shall we have the History out? Do let me know in time that I may prepare to blow the Trumpet of Fame'. He then put his stick in his mouth and in a raree-showman's voice cried, 'Here is the only true History, gentlemen; please to buy, please to buy . . .'. The raree-showman used to bring round peepshows for the pleasure of children in those days. As for the History of Music this was Dr Burney's *magnum opus* of which the last two volumes were published in 1789. There seems to have been quite a spate of histories of music, written by scholars in France, Italy and England besides Dr Burney's mammoth work.

Then finally Fanny married a man in his late fifties when she was forty-one herself. Surprisingly so late in life they had a son and he eventually became a clergyman and died unmarried. That is by the way. What is certain is that the young Fanny looked for a father or a mother in her relationships. Perhaps the early death of her own adored mother gave her a life-long sense of insecurity. Consequently she was inclined to react to situations as her elderly friends did and not as a young girl might be expected to do. Lively, witty and clever she certainly was, but although gifted with these charms, she was painfully reserved and shy, with apparently a need always to do what she thought her father would approve or anyone of her father's generation.

Her early Diary first appeared in print as late as 1889, though it had been started in 1768*. Naturally as a child she was not particularly interested in the fame or social standing of people who came to her parents' home. In fact she did not meet Dr Johnson until 1777 when she was twenty-five and therefore not eligible for this book about children; but her easy style, acute observance of character and natural sense of theatre make for excellent reading, Fanny is never dull.

The Masquerade in January 1770, for instance, must have been typical of many such delightful evening parties given by enterprising hostesses at this period. In this case, however, it was given by Mr Lalauze, the French dancing master, who was married and had a daughter. He was described as 'a very clever Frenchman who had a connection with one of the London theatres'. Hetty Allen, Fanny's step-sister, was of the party and had apparently thought of nothing else for at least three months. Hetty had long decided on her fancy dress, which was that of a Savoyard with a hurdy-gurdy fastened round her waist. Fanny only made up her mind about her own dress by the Friday before the ball. Owing to all the fluster and agitation this indecision had caused she was quite ashamed to go down to the waiting company who had come to see the girls off. There they all were, Captain Pringle, Mr Andrew, the three Miss Pascalls and their father-in-law, Aunt Ann, James, Charles and of course Hetty, so that the parlour was filled. Fanny was glad to be wearing a mask to hide her blushes as they all admired her 'pink Persian vest, covered with gauze in loose pleats and with flowers, etc.' She wore a little garland of flowers on her head. The assembled

*The Early Diary of Fanny Burney, edited by Annie Raine Ellis, 1889.

company repeatedly wished they were going to the party too and so the girls went off in the highest spirits. The Captain handed them into their coach and on their way they collected Mr and Mrs Strange and finally arrived at Leicester Square at the house of their host. Miss Lalauze was sixteen, two years younger than Fanny. Many years before her father Mr Lalauze had performed in a panto-mime given in honour of 'poor Fred', the Prince of Wales at Cliefden (sic). There was a gathering now of many interesting people. Since all of them were in masks they whole-heartedly played up to the impersonations they had chosen. Fanny was in turn accosted by a tall witch, who was obviously a man and who told everyone's fortunes with great success, several nuns, a Punch, a foolish looking shepherd, a Harlequin and a Huntsman, whom Fanny described as suited for nothing but the company of dogs. There was also a Gardener and a Persian, two or three Turks, two Friars and a Merlin, who spoke spells, magic and charms with all the 'mock heroick (sic) and bombast manner which his character could require. Moreover there were two jolly Sailors, many Dominoes and an Indian Queen'. What more could the girls require? What a party it was. A 'very droll old Dutchman' accosted them and amused him-self and them with talking Dutch, though for all Fanny knew he could as well have been speaking Arabic. He made signs of devotion to Fanny, who was characteristically clinging to the protection of a girl dressed as a Nun. Eventually refreshments came and everyone secured a partner, Fanny of course being claimed by the Dutchman and Merlin choosing Hetty. When everybody was unmasked Merlin turned out to be Henry Phipps, the first Earl of Mulgrave and the Dutchman, far from being the 50-year-old fogey Fanny had thought, was a charming young man of twenty-three called Mr Young. He burst out laughing at the sight of Fanny's astonished face and paid her many gallant compliments which clearly were most acceptable. Perhaps the refreshments had thawed her shyness. Fanny noticed with her usual acumen 'the pleasure which appeared in some countenances' after the unmasking ceremony and the dis-appointment in others; seeing 'the old turn young and the young old—in short every face appeared different from what we expected. The old Witch in particular we found was a young officer, the Punch, who had made himself as broad as long, was a very young and handsome man; but what most surprised me was the Shepherd whose own face was so stupid that we could scarcely tell whether he had taken off his mask or not . . . .'.

This masquerade was one Fanny and Hetty never forgot. Years later, in 1779, the diary tells how a younger brother of the Harry

Phipps that Hetty danced with at Mr Lalauze's was brought to visit Mrs Thrale at Streatham.

Shy as she was Fanny was certainly not unsociable. There was nothing she enjoyed more than a ball, and she also attended the theatre, went to innumerable concerts and even watched a cricket match one cold summer. Here she was at a house party and attracted the attention of a member of one of the teams called Mr Gibbs. However, she drily confided to her Journal, 'Mr Gibbs came on my side pretending to screen me from the wind, and entered into small talk with a facility that would not have led me to supposing how high his character stood at the University'. This promising flirtation was noticed by one of the married ladies who enjoyed herself teasing Fanny in whispers, 'Really, Miss Fanny Burney, I don't know what you mean by this behaviour! Oh, girls, girls, girls!' This lady and another talked to her of 'the Captain' the rest of the weekend. Fanny certainly did not lack admirers in her youth. She had no need, like poor Miss Nancy Steele in *Sense and Sensibility* to be continually reminding everybody of her 'beau' the Doctor and his imaginary attentions. She also much enjoyed watching Hetty and Maria Allen's stormy courtships and receiving long confidential letters from the two girls.

By now Fanny is no longer a child, but rising nineteen as the family moves from Poland Street to a charming house in Queen Square. 'It is situated', writes Fanny in November 1770, 'at the upper end of the square and has a delightful prospect of Hamstead and Hygate, we have more than room for our family, large as it is, and all the rooms are well fitted up, convenient and handsome . . .'.

From this house, open on the north side to St George's Fields and Lamb's Conduit, Fanny must have looked towards Highgate and Hampstead villages, standing on the heights, with lovely unspoilt fields between them and Bloomsbury. There we will leave her.

QUEENEY THRALE
1764–1858

Queeney was the eldest child of Dr Johnson's friend Mrs Hester Maria Thrale. If ever a child can be described as literary, whilst never writing any published work, then this was the one. She was brought up knowing well many of the literary lions of the day, like Goldsmith and Fanny Burney, Boswell and above all Dr Johnson, whose pet and correspondent she became, receiving and writing letters to him from a tender age. She also knew Burke, Reynolds, by whom she was painted, and Garrick, as well as many other distinguished people. Johnson liked to call her Queen Esther, hence her pet name Queeney, and he helped with her education and interested himself in all her doings. To be sure she was not always a good correspondent, but she carefully treasured all the letters she received from the great Doctor, jealously guarding them from reading by anybody else during her lifetime. Here is the first one she ever received:

> Ashbourn
> 20 July 1771.

My sweet, dear, pretty, little Miss,

Please to tell little Mama that I am glad to hear that she is well and that I am going to Lichfield and shall come soon to London. Desire her to make haste and be quite well for you know that you and I are to tye her to a tree but we will not do it while she is weak. Tell dear Grandmama that I am very sorry for her pain; Tell Papa that I wish him joy of his new girl* and tell Harry† that you have got my heart and will keep it and that I am

> Dearest Miss
> Your most obedient servant
> Sam: Johnson.

Queeney might almost be considered an infant prodigy, but that so many eighteenth century children reached a very high standard of education at a very early age. She wrote, at ten years old, a volume of 469 pages, called rather formidably, 'An Introduction to the most useful European Languages consisting of Select Passages from the most celebrated English, French, Italian and Spanish authors, with translations as close as possible, so disposed in columns as to give in one view the manner of expressing the same sentence in each language'. However, her tutor Baretti, introduced into the family by Dr Johnson himself, must surely have helped and guided her in this awe-inspiring task. The prose sounds remarkably Johnsonian and unchildlike, though of course children are notoriously good imitators. Years later Queeney kept a diary written in Italian, so she must have been gifted with the ability to learn languages. Baretti wrote that he had been 'teaching Queeney Spanish and Italian from morn till night' during the five-and-a-half years he was tutoring her. Mrs Thrale, by the way, said he was only with them for three years. How difficult for the historian to discover the truth with such conflicting statements.

Latin lessons with Dr Johnson began after Baretti left. Queeney

*Sophia, born July 1771.
†Harry, Mrs Thrale's eldest son now four years old. (He died 1774.)

was twelve years old. Mrs Thrale wrote in her journal, 'Dr Johnson has undertaken to teach my eldest daughter Latin . . . Fanny Burney, mother (sic) of *Evelina* is to learn with her of the same master'. Poor Fanny did not enjoy the lessons but lacked the nerve to tell the Doctor this—She confessed to her Diary, 'I'm sure I fag more for fear of disgrace than for hope of profit'. What Queeney felt is not recorded. Probably she enjoyed her lessons more than Fanny. Johnson announced that she should have two lessons a day instead of one in August, 1780. The following year she was 'working hard at the classics' with her distinguished tutor. She carefully kept the Latin grammar he gave her and the Virgil she inscribed as follows: 'This book was given to H. M. Thrale by Doctor Johnson, 3 April 1783, in Argyle St. It would be valuable as the parting gift of a friend. How much more as of such a friend as Doctor Johnson'.

Apparently Queeney only saw him once more after he had presented her with this book. He died in December 1784 and Fanny Burney reported that 'Miss T' visited him when he was very ill at Bolt Court. Queeney was then just twenty years old.

She must have remembered many happy occasions as she thought back over her childhood. In 1775 there was a Grand Regatta on the Thames. Decorated barges, little yachts with floating streamers, people rowing, 'Merry Andrews' entertaining the company on the banks and a water show at Ranelagh, if you could manage to get a ticket, to end up the day's frolic.

'I was afraid of not being fine enough', wrote Mrs Thrale to Dr Johnson, 'so I trimmed my white lutestring with silver gauze and wore black ribbons intermixed'. Characteristically she did not say what her daughter wore, but she did report that Queeney 'behaved sweetly' and was not afraid of the crowd.

As a matter of fact the outing was not entirely successful because of the bad weather. Dust blew in their faces, rain drove many spectators away from the stands and the wind ruffled the ladies' enormous feather head-dresses and ballooned out their skirts.

Another memory for Queeney was the excitement of the trip to Paris in 1778. It was a kind of birthday treat, as she was celebrating her eleventh birthday three days after they left Dover. Dr Johnson was of the party and he was also celebrating his birthday, reaching the age of sixty-six on 18 September. In fact this was his first and only visit to the Continent. He was always prejudiced against foreigners, in which of course he included the Scots to Boswell's discomfiture. He thought of London as the hub of the Universe and it was indeed his own element. As a tourist, therefore, he was unconscionably insular.

The Thrale-Johnson party had a very disagreeable accident on their way to Paris. In those days such occurrences were fairly common and we remember Parson Woodforde's anxieties on that score whenever he went to a journey. Our company in this case was in two carriages. In one sat Mrs Thrale, an English lady called Mrs Strickland and Dr Johnson. The other was occupied by Mr Thrale, the tutor Joseph Baretti and his pupil Queeney. There must surely have been ladies' maids in attendance, but we are not told about them. The man-servant Sam was mounted unhappily on a bad-tempered horse. What actually caused the upset is rather obscure, but the end of it was that the traces of the carriage broke, one poor horse was run over and the postilion tumbled off his mount. The carriage careered down the hill, causing Mr Thrale to jump out impulsively, landing himself in a chalk pit. He was both hurt and frightened, but luckily the man-servant Sam managed to control his own recalcitrant horse and the carriage was eventually pulled up with no worse mishap. Mrs Thrale, describing the adventure in her journal, was very much disgusted at Johnson's imperturbable deportment, showing 'perfect unconcern for the lives of 3 People'. Baretti assured her that it demonstrated 'true Philosophy', though Mrs Strickland was by no means so charitable. As the carriage that received this shake-up held Baretti, Mr Thrale and Queeney no wonder Mrs Thrale was agitated. Nobody except Johnson reported how the child behaved. 'She loves not me', he said, 'She had not cared for her father. But she certainly did feel for her father when he was hurt'.

Once arrived in Paris they were kept 'very busy in looking about us' and went to Versailles and then to Fontainebleau, where they saw the King and Queen at dinner. This was of course Louis XVI and the unlucky Marie-Antoinette whom they saw. Louis had come to the throne only the year before. Johnson wrote to a friend that 'the Queen was so impressed by "Miss" (Queeney) that she sent one of the gentlemen to inquire who she was'.

In spite of what has been said about his unswerving insularity Dr Johnson's letters to Boswell about this trip to Paris do not sound very uncompromising.

'I will try to speak a little French' he wrote from Calais. '. . . if I heard better I suppose I should learn faster'. He both wrote and understood French excellently, but he was reluctant to speak it, preferring to address Frenchmen in Latin. His letters are full of all the people he saw and the people whom he met and the entertainments he enjoyed.

As for Queeney, she seems to have been included in all the junketings and a very tough child she must have been to face up to all this rubber-necking and what appears to have been remarkably indigestible food, at the age of only eleven. According to Fanny Burney she was shy and reserved but 'fair, round, firm and cherubimical', which is not the sort of description a modern miss would much relish. To Johnson she was 'my sweet, dear, pretty, little miss'. Later on, when she was eighteen, everyone was talking of her beauty. In all his letters to her Dr Johnson wrote full of the warmth of his fatherly love and interest in all that befell her, this child whose mother was never able to waste much love on any of her children. No wonder Queeney treasured and kept the letters which began, 'My dear Charmer, My dearest Love, My dear Sweeting', In 1781 Johnson wrote to her mother, 'I have a mind to look on Queeney as my own dear girl . . .'.

His letters to her were also full of excellent advice and precepts, though he was well aware that he did not always practice what he preached. He resolved that 'if I set her a bad example I ought to counteract it by good precepts'. In one letter he advised her, 'Never delight yourself with the dignity of silence or the superiority of inattention. To be silent or to be negligent are so easy; neither can give any claim to praise, and there is no human being so mean or useless, but his approbation and benevolence is to be desired'. He was probably speaking as much to himself as to his young pupil.

In a lighter vein Queeney signed a joking, mock-legal 'Covenant' in 1774, when she was ten. It was duly sealed, signed and witnessed by Dr Johnson and Mrs Thrale and it had in fact been penned by her tutor Baretti and perhaps the four of them made it up together. This is how it read:

'I do seriously and solemnly promise that from tomorrow forwards I will come down every day (Sunday excepted) at 9 o'clock in the morning to Mr Baretti and read or write whatever Italian he shall bid me during a full hour, but no more. Then to come to him again at 3 o'clock and do the same for another hour and no more. And I promise further that whether I am in good humour or out of humour I will be in earnest and very attentive to my lesson as if I were in the very best humour; nor will I look about me with a vacant and weary countenance, so that the said Mr Baretti (alias Taskmaster) shall have no reason, no not the least shadow of a reason to complain of my disattention, unwillingness and reluctance. And I promise all the above under my hand and seal.'

Dr Johnson's friendship with Mrs Thrale lasted nearly twenty years and his interest in Queeney lasted for the rest of his life. When Mrs Thrale married the music teacher Piozzi in 1784 as 'a

J

rich, gay widow' she had had no less than twelve children by her first husband. Only five of them survived and when their mother followed her new husband to the Continent it was for this desertion of her children that Dr Johnson never forgave her.

One point emerges clearly from the story of Queeney's childhood and that is the extraordinary detachment of Mrs Thrale's attitude towards her children. Their father made her the children's guardian in his will, but he arranged that they should be wards in chancery. For some unknown reason the solicitors let this clause lapse. Perhaps Dr Johnson's continual solicitude for the children had something to do with it. He was appointed as one of the executors of Thrale's will. In any case he felt so strongly when their mother remarried that he broke off a friendship of twenty years. It was not because she was marrying her music teacher Piozzi, however much he and her friends disliked this step, but because she was deserting the children.

As we have seen, Queeney kept Dr Johnson's letters carefully and unlike her mother had no interest in their commercial value. They were lost amongst family papers for many years and only resurfaced a century and a half after they were written, re-discovered amongst a collection of family papers.

Very late in life, at forty-four, Queeney married Admiral the Hon George Keith Elphinstone who became Lord Keith. She was his second wife. But that is another story.

PET MARJORY
1803–1811

One advantage that this remarkable child's story has over most others is that here the authentic child is speaking through her daily journals and we are not listening to an adult reconstruction of what she thought and did.

Marjory Fleming was born in January 1803 and she died before she was nine years old. In the last three years of her life she wrote poems, letters and three journals. One of her editors, Mr Frank Sidgwick, tellingly points out that these comprise the equivalent number of words in the whole of the Gilbert and Sullivan librettos.*

It is worth while putting her against the background of her times. France had declared war on England in 1793 till in 1802 the Peace of Amiens was signed; war broke out again in 1803, this time Bonaparte being our enemy, and this was the year of Marjory's birth.

*The complete Marjory Fleming, her journals, letters and verses, edited by Frank Sidgwick, 1934.

In 1805 came the battle of Trafalgar, and one year later the bill to abolish slavery. No longer would poignant advertisements appear in the newspapers like the one printed in 1768, and quoted by J. H. Plumb in his *England in the Eighteenth Century*. It read, 'To be sold, a fine Negro boy . . . of a sober, tractable, humane disposition, Eleven or Twelve years of Age, talks English very well and can dress Hair in a tollerable (sic) way'. At the beginning of 1800 George, Prince of Wales was not yet forty and he became Regent in 1811, the same year that Marjory died. The whole population of England and Wales was only 11 million. The first census of the population, undertaken by John Rickman, was completed in 1801. Scotland numbered 1,652,000 souls; the population of Glasgow and Edinburgh were each just over 100,000 and London, the gayest, richest city in the world was also the largest in Europe with over a million people.

There was one good thing about life in Scotland when Marjory was born. It was markedly better than it had been at the beginning of the eighteenth century. English farmers and ploughmen had been imported into Scotland to teach new ideas and methods which were accepted very quickly and acted upon by the Scots. Poverty and penury lost their terrors to a great extent and no longer was Doctor Johnson's definition in his dictionary of the word 'oats' quite true. He called it, 'A grain which in England is generally given to horses, but in Scotland supports the people'. Now they were also eating vegetables, cheese and even meat, with a noticeable improvement in their appearance. The tribal system had vanished for ever; the chiefs became lairds instead of war-lords and an increase in education was spread chiefly through the Scottish Society for Promoting Christian Knowledge.

The Scottish capital was famous all over Europe. It boasted remarkable men like Hume and Robertson and a social life of imagination and vigour. The university was also famous. Alas, there were still terrible slums in Edinburgh but new Georgian, classical houses were being built, rather austere in comparison with English Georgian houses, but airy and comfortable. Scotland's wealth was rapidly increasing and although the bad years of the Napoleonic wars caused distress and rising food prices, people no longer died of starvation by hundreds as they had been doing in the first half of the eighteenth century.

Of course this Georgian world into which Marjory was born was a period when child labour was being most shamefully exploited. This lucky child in a well-to-do family, with aristocratic forebears, would have had no idea of how her contemporaries were being treated with such inhumanity. The story of their lives makes horrific reading. Even three-year-olds would be working in the frightening darkness of mines; some, standing up to their ankles in water, pumping, others shut into cells and pulling a string in order to ventilate the pit shafts and others dragging coal trucks. They were aged from three to seven years old and the hordes of friendless, orphaned children were drawn from very poor families or from workhouses like Oliver Twist's terrible orphanage. Let us remember that this was happening all over Europe, not just in our country. To our credit we can also remember that we were leaders in the movement to reform these ghastly conditions, slow though the process was.

Marjory's journals began in Edinburgh when she was visiting the Keiths and immediately we are introduced to her cousin and teacher Isabella Keith, then about seventeen, whom she adored and admired in equal proportions. Marjory's first entry is rather startling. It is 1810, the year of George III's jubilee. 'Many people', she writes, 'are hanged for Highway Robbery, Housebreaking, Murder, etc.' Her first letter is for another Isabella, her elder sister, and it is equally uninhibited, beginning, 'My dear Isa, I now sit down on my botom to answer all your kind and beloved letters which you was so good as to write to me. This is the first time I ever wrote a letter in my Life'. It was not dated, but probably was written before 1809. It continues cheerfully, 'There are a great many Girls in the Square and they cry just like a pig when we are under the painful necessity of putting it to Death'. This mysterious episode is never explained.

Her spelling is delightfully personal, she talks about 'rurel filisity' for instance when she is staying at Braehead, four or five miles west of Edinburgh. The Keith home at Ravelston was nearer, only about two miles out of the capital. All Marjory's journals are carefully corrected by Isabella and the mistakes in spelling underlined. 'There is a dog that yels continualy and I pity him to the bottom of my heart indeed I do'. As the journals were inspired by Isabella as well as corrected by her it is quite remarkable how free they are from selfconsciousness. Certainly they voice a good many moral precepts, presumably for the benefit of Isabella, such as, 'I am very strong and robust and not of the delicate sex nor of the fair but of the deficent in look. People who are deficient (she gets it right this time) in looks can make up for it by virtue'. She sounds such a gay, lively child and admits to liking 'loud mirement and laughter'. Her vivid descriptions have what must be unconscious humour. The story of Isabella's toothache is an example. 'Some days ago Isabella had a tereable fit of the toothake and she walked with a long nightshift at dead of night like a gost and I thought she was one.

She prayed for, tired natures sweet restorer bamy sleep but did not get it a ghostly figure she was indeed enough to make a saint tremble it made me quever and shake from top to toe but soon got the beetter of it and next morning I quite fogot it'. She wrote a poem on George III's birthday which may well have been at the suggestion of Isabella. The muse seems to have come rather late.

'To days ago was the Kings Birthday
And to his healh we sung a lay
Poor man his healh is very bad
And he is often very mad',

Much of the journals are written in verse, and everything has been corrected by Isa Keith for spelling mistakes and almost non-existent punctuation. She reads extraordinarily adult books with great pleasure, like *The Arabian Nights' Entertainments,* which were not written primarily for children, and even Mrs Radcliffe's horrific novel *The Mysteries of Udolpho,* which Isabella Thorpe enjoyed so much in Jane Austen's *Northanger Abbey.*

Sometimes the journals confess to faults. In the summer of 1810 whilst staying blissfully once more at Braehead, Marjory writes, 'I confess that I have been more like a little young Devil that a creature for when Isabella went up the stairs to teach me religion and my multiplication and to be good and all my other lessons I stamped with my feet and threw my new hat which she made on the ground and was sulky and was dreadfully passionate but she never whiped me but gently said Marjory go into another room and think what a great crime you are committing letting your temper git the better of you and I went so sulkely that the Devil got the better of me but she never never whip me . . . To Day I have been very ungrateful and bad and disobedient.'

She seems to have had to enter quite a few misdemeanors during this visit, being naughty in church and 'the very same Divel that tempted Job that tempted me I am sure but he resisted satan though he had boils and many many other misfortunes which I have escaped'. At the end of it all we realise what was behind this temper and irritation. 'I am going to tell you about the horible and wretched plaege that my multiplication gives me you cant concieve it—the most Devilish thing is 8 times 8 and 7 times 7 it is what nature itselfe cant endure'.

Isabella taught her for three or four hours a day in reading, writing and arithmetic 'and many other things and religion into the bargan'. On Sunday she 'teaches me to be virtuous'. This sounds all work and no play to us nowadays, but Marjory's unquenchable enjoyment of

119

life was never damped. She was, like most children, very fond of animals and often describes them. At Braehead there were 'ducks cocks hens bublyjocks (turkeys) 2 dogs 2 cats survive.' She hates the idea of puppies and kittens being drowned and 'would rather have a man dog than a women as they do not bear like women dogs, it is a hard case it is shoking'.

Like Pepys, whose diaries have the same touching quality of truth and honesty and weaknesses for which he was also for ever asking God's forgiveness, Marjory is always hoping she will not incur Isabella's disapproval by bad behaviour. It is a vain hope, as she continues to throw books at her beloved cousin, and then promise to 'turn over a new life', and journal 2 ends with, 'Remorse is the worst thing to bear and I am afraid that I will fall a marter to it'.

Spring 1811 is spent mostly in Edinburgh and later on again she visits Ravelston or Braehead*. One page of the journal is blank except for CARELESS MARJORY. A few pages later 'Miss Potune' makes her appearance, and is described as 'the Simpliton'. She was an 'annibabtist' which Marjory remarks 'is a thing I am not a member of: I am a Pisplikan just now and a Prisbeteren at KerKaldy my native town, which though dirty is clein in the country'. A considerable number of pages are devoted to an appreciation of Cousin Isabella, 'Here lies sweet Isabell in bed with a nightcap on her head . . .'. She also notes that there are a great many balls and routs in Edinburgh and significantly 'the childish distempers are very frequent just now'. Later on she says that a sailor has called to say farewell and she remarks on how dreadful it must be for him to leave his native country 'where he might get a wife or perhaps me, for I love him very much and with all my heart, but O I forgot Isabella forbid me to speak about love'. Another entry, almost the last in the journals, reads, 'God Almighty knows everything that we do or say and he can kill you in a moment'. How poor Isabella must have sorrowed over that sentence, presumably a dictum of her own.

Amongst the poems and letters are many delightful passages, and particularly those addressed to Isabella, the 'Dear little Mama', as she calls her. On her slate Marjory wrote her last poem on Sunday, 15 December 1811, four days before her death. It is addressed to Isabel,

> 'O Isa pain did visit me
> I was at the last extremity'.

*The places are not actually named in the journals.

She went to bed the following Thursday seemingly quite well and then woke and cried 'my head, my head!'

Mr Sidgwick tells us that Dr Geoffrey Keynes considered the most likely cause of her death was meningitis, and as he so justly says it is particularly sad to reflect that her grandfather and two uncles on her mother's side were eminent surgeons.

Marjory's father was an accountant of Kirkcaldy, Fife and on her mother's side she was related to the Raes who moved in literary circles and knew Sir Walter Scott in his youth. She was also related to the family of Keith of Ravelston through her aunt Marianne. There is apparently no proof that she was a favourite with Sir Walter Scott, but as he was a welcome visitor to his Keith cousins probably she met him. In any case Marjory loved his poem Helvellyn and referred to it in her journals.

Whether her early promise would have been fulfilled is debatable, but certainly the charming poems, letters and journals give a vivid and completely genuine picture of the life of a little Regency Scottish girl.

EDWARD LEAR
1812–1888

Since their dates overlap surely Lear and Lewis Carroll must have known each other's work, but it is quite possible that since Lear grew up and developed in the Regency period he did not favour the logical, mathematical, if poetical, approach to nonsense that Carroll's masterpieces are illuminated by: Lear's work in any case cannot be compared in stature to Carroll's. What they shared was a love of children and considerable loneliness of heart and eccentricity of behaviour. Surely Lear has more in common with W. S. Gilbert's nonsense in the Bab Ballads.

Lear was the youngest of an incredibly large and prosperous family of a stockbroker numbering no less than 21 children. Those important early years were happy ones. He was fond of recalling his earliest memory, in 1815 aged three, when he believed he remembered being wrapped up in a blanket and taken out of his cot to see the fireworks celebrating Waterloo. In fact he was particularly proud of his memory and swore he could remember 'every particle' of his life from the tender age of four. He had nothing very pleasant to remember when he was seven as he then started the horrible epilepsy attacks which he referred to as the 'Terrible Demon' which dogged him throughout his life. He shunned strangers and was never so much at ease with adults as with children. What with his bad sight, ugly appearance and chronic asthma and bronchitis the wonder was he did not become utterly 'mad, bad and sad', as he put it. When he was thirteen his rich father became bankrupt and was imprisoned so the disaster affected all the family. Mrs Lear entrusted Edward to one of his older sisters, Anne and the rest of the family was split up. So Edward learnt everything he knew from this sister, since his bad health prevented him from attending school. So clever a draughtsman did he become that by fifteen he was earning a living drawing medical records of diseases for doctors and hospitals. His gay drawings of later years are the skilled antics from the pen of a brilliantly accurate student, who produced magnificent and detailed coloured lithographs of parrots for the zoo in 1832 when he was still only twenty. This year also saw the birth of our other famous nonsense writer, Lewis Carroll. A few years later Lear illustrated a book on *Tortoises, Terrapins and Turtles* written by J. E. Gray of the British Museum. The artist's brilliant draughtsmanship was an immediate success and subsequently came a commission from the Earl of Derby to illustrate his book about his own private menagerie. This book appeared in 1846, the year when Queen Victoria, impressed by his drawings, commanded his presence at Osborne where he gave her a course of 12 drawing lessons—Lear, about forty years later, still glowed at the thought of the Queen '. . . I don't know if its proper to call a sovereign a duck', he wrote, 'but I cannot help thinking H.M. a dear and absolute duck'.

The year 1846 was indeed a year of triumphs for Lear, as his *First Book of Nonsense* was also published. The difference between the meticulously realistic zoological illustrations and the gay caricatures of the nonsense book which posterity remembers him by, show the other side of his genius. It is fascinating to see the talented artist deliberately simplifying his drawings to please his young friends. The inspiration apparently came from either the Francillon children or from Lord Derby's grandchildren. As we have seen, the *First Book of Nonsense* came out in the same year as the book on the menagerie in 1846.

Lear wrote for children to escape from himself and his worries and the cruelty and lack of sympathy of an unfeeling world. Perhaps that is the invaluable gift of nature to the sensitive artist. Lear mocked his own ugliness, his restlessness, his bad sight, his insecurity. He was terrified of dogs, and so many of his drawings of these animals are over man-size. His delight in coining words and playing with language is a characteristic he shared with Lewis Carroll. Besides limericks, which by the way he did not invent but popularised, he wrote other forms of nonsense and the 'Owl and the Pussycat' poem

Edward Lear as he saw himself in his own pen-and-ink drawing, 1862–63. Courtesy of the National Portrait Gallery.

was written to entertain John Addington Symond's three-year-old daughter, whom he met in 1868, wintering at Cannes. Lear brought the child pictures or poems nearly every day, Symonds told a friend. He gave the birds he drew nonsensical names, caricaturing the exotic parrots and macaws he had so meticulously represented in his book for the zoo. Another child, this time a little boy called Hubert Congrave the son of a schoolmaster living at San Remo appeared next. For Hubert Lear brought drawings of flowering plants and when he went to dinner with the Congreves he would invent non-sense menus, both subjects appearing later under the title of *Nonsense Songs, Stories, Botany and Alphabets.* Hubert Congreve considered Lear to be 'my dearest and best friend of the older generation'. Another of this long line of child friends of Lear's was called Margaret Terry. She was the daughter of an American artist who was passing the summer in a hotel near Turin up in the moun-tains. Margaret told her mother she wished Lear were her uncle, which naturally delighted him and he insisted upon being called henceforward 'adopty duncle'. They walked together in the mountains and every day he laid a drawing on her plate at dinner which illustrated a letter of the alphabet.

Like Carroll, Lear played with words to the delight of himself and generations of children, who enjoyed the wild improbabilities of his imagination. What child could resist a plant called Minspysia Deliciosa; or the Great Gromboolian Plain, where the sorrowful Dong with the Luminous Nose lived; or Lady Jingly from the Coast of Coromandel. The limerick which introduces *The First Book of Nonsense* published in 1846 may have been referring to the Derby children, or to the Francillon children, who claimed to have owned many of the original drawings and limericks. It bears quoting as at once an introduction and an epitaph to Edward Lear:

> 'There was an old Derry down Derry,
> Who loved to see little folks merry;
>   So he made them a Book
>   Till with laughter they shook,
> At the fun of that Derry down Derry.'

LEWIS CARROLL
(Charles Lutwige Dodgson)
1832–1898

A bachelor, an academic and an ascetic, Carroll was an extremely religious-minded clergyman, which is not always in history a characteristic of the cloth. He was also a retiring, quiet man. His fame rests on his books written for children in a language few children understand perfectly until they are grown-up. Although the Alice books were well-known in his lifetime, only after his death did his fame slowly gather momentum until thirty years after his death Sotheby's sold the manuscript of his original version of *Alice in Wonderland* for the considerable sum of £15,400. The following year the buyer re-sold his treasure for nearly double this figure to an American. Then, after the 1940 World War, this same American, Mr Eldridge R. Johnson, helped by other Americans, gave the manuscript to the British Museum by way of a tribute of appreciation to Great Britain for their part in World War II. This generosity puts us all in his debt.

G. M. Young has pointed out that a 'new, unpietistic handling of childhood' took place in the mid-nineteenth century and Carroll, no less than Edward Lear, the nonsense poet, exemplifies this trend. Alice is above all a child of sterling common sense, considerable dignity and courage and of course with great wit and

This charming drypoint of girls playing croquet is by James Joseph Tissot, reminiscent of Lewis Carroll's famous croquet match in *Alice in Wonderland*. Courtesy of Sotheby's.

gaiety. She is a true-to-life child and not a stock figure of childhood. There are no godly remarks or pious moralising here; the Alice books follow that long line of an English speciality, the nonsense book, which is at best as old as Shakespeare. This vein running through these books is what Chesterton called 'a satisfaction of the fancy'. As Humpty Dumpty remarked, 'there's glory for you'. However, don't try to explain it, or it will disappear under dissection like the Cheshire Cat's smile.

Play on words has long been an English pastime; look up your Shakespeare. The French had a soft spot for this type of wit in the nineteenth century which certainly the English of the same period shared. Alice is a far cry from the children's books of the past intended to instruct and edify. These books were written simply to give pleasure and they are surely amongst the immortals.

Carroll must have inherited his nonsense wit from his father, who wrote to him at the age of eight . . . 'What a bawling and tearing of hair there will be! Pigs and babies, camels and butterflies, rolling in the gutter together—old women rushing up the chimneys and cows after them—ducks hiding themselves in coffee cups and fat geese trying to squeeze themselves into pencil cases . . . '. Remember the Dormouse in *Alice in Wonderland* being stuffed into the teapot? Other childhood memories figure in his books; the child's 'left-hand shoe' hidden under the nursery floor at Darlington appears in the White Knight's story. The agéd, agéd man was recalled to his memory if, amongst other peculiar acts, he 'madly thrust a right-hand foot into a left-hand shoe'. Perhaps Lewis's wretched years at Rugby and the shock of his mother's early death sent him searching for 'those evenings long ago' when he was a child. In spite of his scholastic brilliance and success he could write at twenty-one:

> 'I'd give all wealth that years have piled,
> The slow result of Life's decay,
> To be once more a little child
> For one bright summer day'.

Lewis Carroll certainly remained obsessed with his early years, a child in some respects all his life. But remember that he was reported as having been remarkable for maturity of mind as well as his sensitivity at the age of twelve. His stammer may have caused him to seek the uncritical society of children for relaxation. In his youth he was tireless in his efforts to amuse his brothers and sisters with imaginative games, manuscript magazines, drawings, stories, and poems. His childhood seems to have been extremely happy till he went to Rugby and his mother died. Perhaps his

Charles Lutwidge Dodgson, alias Lewis Carroll, drawn by Harry
Furness. Courtesy of the National Portrait Gallery.

devotion to children, becoming not only an immortal writer for them but the best photographer of them in the nineteenth century, kept this complex and original character a child himself at heart.

Carroll 'gathered together loose ends of fancy and experience that stretched back many years.' Parody was a *genre* he had used since childhood when he wrote his magazines, poetry and diaries.

His friendship with Alice Liddell, the original of the Alice books, one of the daughters of the Dean of Christchurch, is very important. He first met her in April, 1856 when he was twenty-four, and Alice only four, but prophetically he wrote in his diary, 'I mark this day with a white stone'. This comment was only used for red-letter-days. Her brother Harry and her sisters Louisa and Edith and Alice herself passed that famous afternoon on the river with Carroll and his friend Robinson Duckworth in July 1862. The story of Alice began as an impromptu entertainment and in the following six months he wrote the story at the particular request of Alice. Eventually it was revised for publication, and John Tenniel drew his immortal illustrations for it. The original manuscript in the British Museum does not contain the later improvements of 'Pig and Pepper' and 'a Mad Teaparty' nor the delightful parodies 'Twinkle, twinkle little bat', "Tis the voice of the Lobster', 'Will you walk a little faster' and 'Speak roughly to your little Boy'. Mr Derek Hudson tells us that Lewis Carroll was himself the Dodo, his friend Duckworth the Duck, Louisa figured as the Lory, Edith was the Eaglet and Alice herself of course. Which character Harry took we do not know. The Dormouse's story about the treacle well shows the three little girls in another disguise, Elsie, Lacie and Tilly respectively standing for L.C. (Louisa Charlotte); Alice, in anagram; and Edith's nickname Matilda or Tillie. The 'funny, pretty book'* had an immediate success, read by both children and adults ever since. Its timeless appeal reaches most of us and is certainly now a part of our national folk-lore. This curiouser and curiouser dream-world created by Lewis Carroll is completely acceptable and his well-concealed art also disguises a sense of purpose beneath the wit and entertainment. Alice learns unconsciously lessons on how to live not only in the mad world of her dream, but in the true world. She emerges able to sympathise with all kinds of oddities, to stand on her own feet and to speak her own mind fearlessly as well as to put up philosophically with eccentricity. Moreover, she learns how important words are, and how to use them carefully. Carroll revived several words that had been forgotten;

*Christina Rosetti.

for instance, the poem about the Jabberwock re-introduced beamish, slithy and burbled. His own contribution to the dictionary were two new words from the same poem, galumphing and chortle. Sentences from *Alice Through the Looking-Glass* like 'jam tomorrow and jam yesterday but never jam today' have become part of our language too, and also 'as large as life and twice as natural'.

Although his own life was not altogether happy, his golden childhood has enriched the lives of other children through his books. He died aged sixty-six in 1898. Young and old all over the world, where his books have been translated, will go on laughing and enjoying his nonsense.

CHAPTER SEVEN

Royal Children

Queen Anne's record for child mortality can hardly have been surpassed in royal circles. She had ten miscarriages, four children who did not survive infancy and one son who lived until he was 11 years old. She was, of course, the daughter of James II and Anne Hyde and her reign began at the very start of the eighteenth century. This period is considered by historians to be the pinnacle of infant mortality, the toll of child life continuing well into the nineteenth century. Dr Hans Sloane, a famous eighteenth century physician, opposed the 'by hand' feeding of babies, considering that the refusal of mothers to breast feed their children was the main cause of infant deaths. Half of these deaths were of children under two, and they were mostly caused by wrong feeding. The doctor was one of the foundation governors of the Foundlings Hospital which was created in 1748. Rich mothers also refused to nurse their babies.

In the upper classes there were great contrasts in children's upbringing. The little Wesleys were given austere meals of 'spoon meat', taught to 'fear the rod' and systematically cowed into slavish obedience. On the other end of the scale Charles James Fox's father was determined that his son's spirits should not be broken. He said, 'the world will do that business fast enough'. There is a legend that Charles was allowed to ride on a saddle of mutton at a tender age, his feet splashing about in the gravy. Permissiveness, one feels, could hardly go further.

It was Wesley's methods, however, which set the rules for most children for the following 100 years. We have to remember that although nowadays there is practically no distinction in clothes between the Lord High Chancellor in the box and the Lord High Beggarman in the stocks. In the eighteenth century, and also in the nineteenth century, children who attended Sunday school or outings planned by the Band of Hope, for example, would have been immediately recognised by their clothes. These differentiated them from the squire's children. In 1900 even the cottage children wore black woollen stockings and thick-soled boots, often nailed. A carved wooden child's boot, about life-size for a baby of two, was made as a collecting box for the Raggéd Schools in the last century. It is so worn that a mouse peers out of a tear in the 'leather'. What an amusing bygone to find at a market-stall; or is it a bit too near the truth to bear thinking about?

However, we must return to the Hanoverians who followed Queen Anne. George I came to the throne in 1714, none of Anne's children having survived her; and both he and his son were essentially Germans, for George I never attempted to speak English and spent at least half of each year out of the country in his beloved Hanover. George II lived mostly outside London at Richmond. The reason for this, it was often said, was because driving through the muddy streets of Brentford reminded him of Hanover.

George I brought over a strange retinue of fat and far from attractive mistresses, of whom Melusina von der Schulenburg, Duchess of Kendall was the only one who took the trouble to learn English. No wonder the Jacobites imagined their uprising in 1715, under the Earl of Mar, would succeed with such unattractive rivals on the throne. As George I had no Queen, social life revolved round his son and the clever, capable Caroline of Anspach, who was his son's wife.

Feuds were customary amongst the Hanoverians. George I quarrelled with his son, who in turn quarrelled with 'Poor Fred', his first-born. Prince Frederick reacted violently to his father's dislike and never told his parents that his wife was expecting a baby in 1737 in July. Instead he deliberately allowed them to believe that the birth would not be until October. The consternation and turmoil that ensued, resulting in the arrival of Princess Augusta at 11.30 pm on 31 July at St James's was horrific. No beds had been prepared for the sudden arrival of the expectant Princess of Wales, who was driven from Hampton Court at the double and perforce given tablecloths on the bed instead of sheets. The Queen thought they were still at Hampton Court and when a Lady-in-waiting dashed into her bedroom to announce the birth, the poor Queen thought the palace was on fire. The whole affair ended in a lasting breach between the King and the Prince of Wales. Eventually poor Fred died of a rather unromantic rupture resulting from a blow he sustained from a cricket ball. Since sport of various kinds had been his main interest his end was in keeping with his life, it seems.

Fred's wife brought up her son, later to become George III, in a restricted family circle at Kew as far away as possible from his dissolute grandfather's court. George II's manners were gauche to the point of rudeness and he shouted at the young princesses at the slightest sign of misbehaviour, even taking off his wig and kicking it about like a football to vent his spleen. Rough and ill-mannered as he was to his wife Caroline, he was stricken with grief and remorse when she died, and left Hampton Court for Kensington where memories of her were less evident.

The good-natured cheerful George III, with his religious and abstemious habits, came to the throne at twenty-three and he was the complete opposite of his father and grandfather. In 1760 he made a Speech from the Throne in which he said, 'I glory in the name of Britain and the peculiar happiness of my Life will ever consist in promoting the Welfare of a people whose Loyalty and warm affection for me I consider as the greatest and most permanent Security of my Throne'. The King took a vegetarian diet and the Queen liked her German sausages. They both enjoyed porridge for breakfast and life at Court was frugal to a degree unheard of before amongst Hanoverians. It is said that our famous Apple-Charlotte pudding was an invention of the Queen's to use up odds and ends of bread and prevent waste. The sad thing was that the great British public did not like to see their Royalty practising strict economies and living the life of an ordinary English squire. They preferred a bit of show and extravagance and goodness knows they were going to get it when Prinny succeeded his father. Meanwhile, the princes assembled at Kew from their separate houses for breakfast at eight every morning and the princesses, under the tutelage of Miss Goldsworthy and the vigilant Queen and Lady Charlotte Finch, who was no more than nominal head of the household, learnt languages, French, German and Italian, needlework and music. They were to be educated to take their places in life later on as wives of 'minor Continental Princes'. That was the plan, and out of the six only three married, as luck would have it. King George, who was supposed to be overseeing his sons' education, never seems to have visited the school-room. The discipline there was practically non-existent and the foundation of a love of wine and women and gambling is often said to have been cradled at Kew.

Thirteen of the King's fifteen children reached maturity, seven boys and six girls. They all lived at Kew, the boys having three separate houses with their tutors. George had always admired Eton, but he preferred to have his sons educated at home and then five of them were sent to Hanover to 'finish'. Only George IV and William IV were educated entirely in the English way.

Although he never visited the school-room, or so we are told, nevertheless George took an interest in building model farms with them and encouraging both the boys and the girls to play 'stump-cricket', football and hockey. This must have been a very happy period for poor George III when the children were no problem and would ride out on horseback or in carriages whilst the populace watched, curtseying and taking off their hats in greeting. The children were a fine looking group. It was only much later that the boys became so overweight and unattractive. Later in their adolescence George III showed a harshness and authoritarianism quite unlike the kindly interest he showed his children in the days at Kew.

In 1771 the Earl of Holdernesse was put in charge of the two eldest princes, eight and nine years old. Horace Walpole called him 'a solemn phantom'. A tutor, William Markham, Bishop of Chester, was also chosen, and Dr Cyril Jackson was appointed his assistant. Both were good scholars, particularly Jackson, but Markham seems to have maintained a fierce discipline, taking literally the King's order, 'If they deserve it, let them be flogged'.

In 1776, when the princes were thirteen and fourteen years old, the quarrels between Markham and the Governor, Lord Holdernesse, grew acute and the King appointed Lord Bruce to be governor, and the Bishop of Worcester, Richard Hurd, superseded Markham. Hurd was a lively, amusing, human man and a good judge of boys too. One of his reports on fifteen year old Prinny read, 'He will become either the most polished Gentleman or the most accomplished blackguard in Europe—possibly both'. The Prince of Wales appears to have been a timid child and uninterested in martial games. By seven he was already at loggerheads with his father. 'He hates me. He always did, from the age of seven', he is reported as saying, when he was in his twenties. Certainly George III was no exception to the custom of strife between Hanoverian fathers and sons, which we have already noted. Later the King accused his twelve year old son of evasion, duplicity and untruthfulness. The impression the young Prince made on others was of great charm and even good looks. His first love was one of his sister's governesses, for whom he expressed deep affection when he was only sixteen. This was the beginning of a life-long series of affairs of the heart, and it seems as though all his loves were always considerably older than himself. He admitted in a billet-doux to his first love, that he was 'rather too fond of wine and women', which seems touchingly naïve in a boy of sixteen to our present way of thinking.

A few weeks after this letter, in which he drew a self-portrait, he transferred his volatile affections to another, four years older than

himself. This beautiful lady* encouraged the young Prince and when, after a year, the inevitable cooling off occurred, she brazenly demanded £5,000 for his love-letters. This did not, of course, help the relationship between the King and his son.

However, the Prince was no fool and seems to have enjoyed languages both ancient and modern, speaking fluently German, French and Italian and quoting easily from Latin and Greek poets. He liked literature†, music (playing the 'cello himself) and he appreciated the arts. At eighteen he became heir apparent and, with the end of his childhood, here we take leave of him.

Prince Frederick, Duke of York, had no intellectual interests. Only one year younger than Prinny and automatically destined for the army, he took to it enthusiastically.

The next two brothers, William, Duke of Clarence, and Edward, Duke of Kent, became eventually, one William IV and the other Queen Victoria's father. William went to sea at the age of thirteen as midshipman. His father insisted that he should be given 'no marks of distinction'. Nevertheless the King expected the boy to continue his classical studies and he was given a private study and accompanied by a tutor, who was rather eccentrically granted the title of 'honorary midshipman'. William not only enjoyed practical jokes, a tendency amongst our Hanoverian sovereigns that lasted at least until Edward VII, but he was 'handy with his fists'. He saw a good deal of active service at this tender age. Back home at fifteen, on leave his elder brothers saw to it that he was initiated into their own style of dissipation. He was entangled on one occasion with a sixteen year old girl, and George III sent him immediately back to sea. One of his instructors was Nelson, who spoke well of him, but he was too independent and impulsive for a service man though he became a Captain at twenty-three, where we must leave him.

Queen Victoria's father, Edward of Kent, was yet another uncontrollable son of poor George III. Dr John Fisher, later Bishop of Salisbury, who tutored the two young Princes, reported a conversation that gives a picture of Edward's uncompromising

*Mrs Perdita Robinson.
†Reading profusely; Byron, Scott and Jane Austen for example.

◀ Commemorative Scottish pottery plates of George IV and Queen Caroline. The George IV plate published in 1820–21 to celebrate his accession to the throne, the Caroline plate of the same date to further the Whig support of the Queen in the *Bill of Pains and Penalties*. Photograph by Jennifer May.

honesty and equally uncompromising impulsiveness. He smashed a valuable clock treasured by his father. Asked about it he replied, 'Yes, I did it'. 'But your Royal Highness did it by accident?' 'No, I did it intentionally'. 'But your Royal Highness regrets what you have done?' 'No, not at all'.

He was, one is not surprised to learn, by no means his parents' favourite child. Off he went at seventeen to Hanover, like William, but he was to be trained as a soldier. The Hanoverian characteristics appeared in yet another form. He was extravagant, rebellious, but, in some ways, dependable and even efficient; almost too efficient, one suspects. His stern and cruel discipline nearly caused a mutiny at Gibralter and he was forced to leave this post; yet, in ordinary life, he was said to have been amicable and kind.

The three junior brothers never seem to have rebelled against their father so much as the elder four. The youngest of all, Prince Adolphus, was George III's favourite, and these three were all sent to the University of Göttingen for a German finish to be put on their education. There they imbibed moral and experimental philosophy, mathematics, geography and history. Classics seem to have been left out except for Augustus who profited from Mr Hayne, his tutor at the University. Out of all his seven sons George III had only one scholarly one and this was Augustus, Duke of Sussex. He spent a good part of his formative years wintering in Italy because of his asthma, a well-known anxiety symptom, and this period laid the foundation for his love of books. He amassed an enormous library, and his collection of Bibles alone amounts to over 5,000 different varieties. He also acquired a splendid collection of manuscripts of Italian operas.

The youngest Prince, Adolphus, Duke of Cambridge, was also gifted with an interest in learning and he became an excellent linguist. These seven sons were mostly over six feet tall, but only one of them did not grow stout in later years. Their passion for gambling, eating, drinking and roistering was notorious and a more headstrong and self-willed group it would be hard to find. Yet they were adored by their sisters and had many talents, social, intellectual and musical.

As for the six Princesses, their early days were comparatively virtuous, whatever their later years may have brought. They were described, perhaps rather sycophantically, by Fanny Burney. 'Never in tale or fable', she wrote, 'were six sister Princesses more lovely'. However, since less biassed witnesses have all corroborated this opinion, they must have had great charm and even wit, nor did they cause their governesses much trouble or concern.

The Princesses played cricket and football with their brothers, as we have seen, and they reluctantly joined their parents on trips in the royal yacht. They enjoyed dances and parties and country visits and they learnt foreign languages and such accomplishments of their day and age as beadwork, netting purses and embroidery; painting and ancient history. The lady who supervised their activities for 30 years was Lady Charlotte Finch. Even Horace Walpole, whose sharp tongue is well known, had nothing but praise for her. 'The cleverest girl in the world', he called her. She managed to combine all her duties with marriage and her own social life, nor did she neglect her intellectual interests.

Miss Jane Gomm was on duty to watch over the Princesses' meals, lessons, manners and behaviour and Fanny Burney reports that she was 'very sensible and well informed'; but she adds that 'her manner is not pleasing to strangers'. Miss Gomm shared her duties with her 'twin dragon of decorum', Miss Caroline Goldsworthy. Both were of course under the command of Lady Charlotte Finch. Many under-governesses came and went.

Not one of these six unhappy Princesses made normal happy marriages; chiefly because, like their brothers, they fell in love with commoners. Girls, however, could not be permitted to indulge in free love, more especially if they were Princesses. The Princess Royal escaped from her parents' roof, which she nicknamed 'the cloister', by marrying a middle-aged Hereditary Prince who had lost his first wife. Lost is indeed the operative word, since the first Princess of Würtemberg disappeared in peculiar circumstances. This second marriage was childless; the royal bride was thirty-one. Princess Mary married 'Silly Billy', who was the Duke of Gloucester, and Princess Elizabeth married, when she was forty-seven, a far from attractive German princeling, the Landgrave of Hesse-Hornburg. The other three daughters of George III never married.

THE FAMILY OF QUEEN ADELAIDE
1793–1849

A Spanish gypsy once told the Duke of Kent that he was destined to be the father of a great Queen. Like the Delphic oracle this was an utterance with a certain amount of latitude, but the Duke interpreted it to mean that his future child would be Monarch of England. So, in 1816 he borrowed £1,000 from the Tsar and off he went to Baden to search for a likely Princess. Both he and his brother, the Duke of Clarence, were heavily in debt and the promise of government generosity, if they married and left their longstanding mistresses and children, tipped the scales. These elderly Romeos went to look for brides. The Duke of Clarence had ten children with their education on his hands and his debts were in the range of £56,000. He bargained with the government for £12,000 down and £30,000 a year on his marriage. The Duke of Cambridge also wanted a wife. The choice, chiefly on religious grounds, was limited.

To be sure, the three Princes were not very eligible. Clarence was fifty-three and so odd were his manners, with his custom of swearing so horribly, that the wife of the Russian Ambassador reported him to be 'the least educated of all the English princes'. She added that his manners, conversation and habits were vulgar to say the least. This would not have worried his compatriots who had no use for elegant continental ways. In any case William was a bluff, breezy sailor who hated foreigners. However, he told his brother Cambridge to keep a weather eye open for a bride for him when he was in Germany. After many ups and downs, in which several offers were made to ladies on William's behalf, the choice was whittled down to two Princesses. The 18-year-old Princess Caroline refused, through her father, due to the bridegroom's ripe age and numerous children. So the last hope was Princess Adelaide of Saxe Meiningen. She was twenty-five with the most amiable and warm nature imaginable, as well as being intelligent and religious-minded; but she certainly was no beauty. Well, nor was poor pineapple-headed William. However, the long and the short of it was that this delightful young woman decided that as a Princess she had no other way out of the small restricted circle of her father's Court than by marriage. So in April, 1818, just five months before Princess Charlotte's death in childbirth, William announced his engagement. It was an act of duty, Canning announced to Parliament. When he continued that the Duke's reason was to 'provide for a succession to the throne' there was loud, rude laughter.

Princess Adelaide's reception by her mother-in-law-to-be was far from agreeable. Queen Charlotte had six daughters-in-law of whom the worst by far was Prinny's Queen Caroline and the best, as it turned out, Princess Adelaide, whom Queen Charlotte herself had picked out for William. The ugly old Queen received Adelaide at Kew Palace and gave her the benefit of a long and disagreeable homily about William's debts and his paltry income, which she herself, due to her straitened circumstances, could in no way augment. She also made it clear that neither William's wedding nor the Duke of Kent's could be celebrated by any form of entertaining on account of the expense. The Prince Regent found it quite out of the question to give any Balls or Soirées for them and they must leave for Germany directly after the wedding ceremony.

Good, kind-hearted Adelaide received all these remarks with courtesy and equanimity, but on one point she was adamant. The old Queen did not relish the idea of the deplorable gaggle of Fitz-Clarence children joining the bride's household. They would be most unsatisfactory companions for any little grandchild that Adelaide and William might produce. Adelaide, however, was determined to take on the ten Fitz-Clarence stepchildren. It would be a rugged duty but she was satisfied that she must befriend them. William, however, was forced by his mother not to allow them to attend his wedding. Perhaps this was a blessing in disguise. They were notoriously ill-mannered and boisterous. Adelaide had nothing to fear from their mother, the ageing actress Dorothea Jordan, who was nearly five years older than the Duke. Many of the Fitz-Clarences were now grown up and married, so what it amounted to was that kind Adelaide took over the care of the four youngest girls of William's alliance with the former highly successful actress Dorothea Jordan. Dora was friendly and gay, 'the child of nature to hear whom laugh was to drink nectar'. William had met her when he was twenty-six and she thirty and already she had a motley crew of children by other men to look after. Her life does not belong in this book, but of all her troupe of lovers not one of them stood in Paris by her grave to mourn her when she died in 1815.

Soon after marriage the royal couple set off for Hanover, significantly being sent in the second-best yacht. This was in 1818. Queen Charlotte died in November and there was a huge funeral, in spite of the fact that the old lady had never liked the British people any more than they liked her. Nor did the Duke of Clarence waste any tears. He had the excuse of not attending the obsequies because Adelaide was expectant. The same applied to Kent, Cumberland and Cambridge. The Prince Regent was the only one of her sons who sincerely mourned the Queen.

Alas, Adelaide lost her baby and nearly died herself. William nursed her devotedly, to the surprise of all his relatives. Clearly he had truly fallen in love. Meanwhile the Duchess of Kent produced 'a pretty little princess as plump as a partridge'.

The new royal nurseries were filling up quickly; both the Duchess of Cambridge and the Duchess of Cumberland produced boys and the two children were both confusingly called George. Quickly Adelaide was again expectant and they returned to England so that she might be under the care of the Regent's doctor. The royal couple travelled over the roads in appalling weather from Lieben-stein to Louisbourg and thence to Homburg, and Ghent and on to Dunkirk, intending to take a yacht to England. The result was that Adelaide had a miscarriage on reaching Dunkirk. Unselfish, as ever, the poor Duchess insisted they leave for England after only a few days and consequently Dover was as far as she could get before she collapsed for six weeks at Lord Liverpool's castle, which, as it happened, was very draughty and cold. After this they moved into William's bachelor flat in St James's.

In 1820 Adelaide and William settled into a house near Hampton Court, where he had lived for so many years with Dorothea Jordan. Anyone far less sweet-natured than Adelaide might have been forgiven for detesting the very idea of such a home, more especially since it contained the unruly young Fitz-Clarences, who naturally enough regarded this house at Bushey as their true home. William's touching desire that his 'superior-minded Princess' should accept the stepchildren was only equalled by her desire to do well by them. All of them had been given the names of their royal relations. George, with his colossal appetite, was in the army and now married; so he was no problem. Adolphus was a sailor but sounds far from pre-possessing with 'vast pouch-like chops'. He was not at home either, of course. Frederick was a soldier and considered to be the best of the brood. He was away when his father married in 1818 and subsequently he was created Earl of Munster and became an *aide-de-camp* to Queen Victoria. Another boy, Henry, had died abroad in India. That left six children for Adelaide to mother. 'Princess Sophia of Jordan', as she was aptly called, was the same age as her stepmother, Mary was 21, Elizabeth was 19, Augusta 17, Augustus 15 and Amelia, the youngest, was 13. What a handful for a young woman to take over.

Excellent though Adelaide's sweetness and goodness were, it does look rather like masochism to hang Dorothea Jordan's portrait over the mantelpiece, especially after William had tactfully re-moved it in case it gave offence. Adelaide, however, discovered that the picture had always hung in this place and since it was a likeness of her stepchildren's mother she thought it only right that it should remain in its old place. Adelaide's constant pre-occupation was to sweeten the sour relationships of her in-laws and she started sensibly enough in her own home.

William was very pleased when the eldest Fitz-Clarence son produced a grand-daughter for him and she was given the name of Adelaide. Alas, his own daughter, born two months later and called Elizabeth, died of convulsions when only three months old, which catastrophe was caused by 'an entanglement of the bowels'. Poor Adelaide carried a statue of her sleeping child, lying on a tiny chaise-longue, with her for the rest of her life.*

This remarkable Princess must have had the character of a saint, for she never allowed her grief and disappointment to cloud her relationship with other people's children. Little Princess Victoria of Kent was one of her favourites and she wrote letters to her on many occasions, calling the future Queen her 'dear, dear little Victoria'. It is comforting to know that one at least of her stepchildren, Captain Fitz-Clarence, referred to her as 'the best and most charming woman in the world'.

PRINCESS CHARLOTTE
1796–1817

Charlotte's parents were first cousins. Whether this fact affected her health and character of course cannot be proved, but she had 'the Brunswick family stutter and a lop-sided stance' and if we are to believe Creevey, she not only suffered from a 'fixed pain in her side' but she wore a 'perpetual blister' to cure it. An hereditary tendency to trouble in the knee and the side was certainly a legacy from her papa's side of the family as three of his sisters suffered from these misfortunes. The aunts, it appears, were devoted to her and so were her grandparents George III and Queen Charlotte. Aunt Libby reported that when she was staying with them all at Weymouth in 1797 she prayed for 'Papa, Mama, Charlotte and fleas'. This slip of the tongue, for she had meant 'friends' of course, was due to her having been severely bitten by fleas the night before. Her governess-in-chief Lady Elgin thought the word should be vetoed, but Miss Hayman, one of the younger governesses, of whom there were many, answered, 'Why, Madam, you know we are told to pray for our enemies, and surely the fleas are the only ones HRH has!' Let us hope Lady Elgin was amused. It is of some social interest to note that professional flea-catchers were in fact employed regularly 'to free the royal bedding from these intruders'.

Charlotte's life at this stage was touchingly idyllic. The King gave her a large rocking-horse which, said Aunt Libby, gave her much pleasure and thankfulness. In 1804 she wrote to her eldest aunt, who had sent her many delightful toys from Louisburg, including a dolls' tea-set, 'I hope to go to Windsor soon, and see my dear Grandpapa and Grandmama, I love very much to go and play with my aunts'. The aunts did misrepresent the fondness and

*This statue is now at Windsor Castle.

paternal devotion of their brother George for his offspring. The customary meetings of father and daughter at the breakfast table bored the Prince, and it certainly wasn't the ideal time of day to meet his child, knowing the life he led. Nevertheless, he was credited with being 'good with children' generally. He was kind to little Minnie Seymour and to his young niece Victoria. His own child, however, always maintained that he disliked her and in his presence she was usually silent and sullen so that her aunts said her father never saw her in her true colours. The picture of the relationship is contradictory, for he certainly gave his daughter delightful gifts, like the beautiful Italian greyhound and charming pieces of jewellery. To give him his due he had made several attempts to interest himself in his young daughter and she was brought to converse with him over his breakfast of broiled bones, soda water and Dalby's Carminative, a remedy much used by dissipated rakes to aid recovery after a night's roistering, being a specific against 'inward risings'. Occasionally he had an impulse of rather easy generosity, offering the child this beautiful Italian greyhound which he had been given, saying 'I don't care for dogs, but . . . Charlotte loves them'.

The child's manners, not unsurprisingly, as she was after all her mother's daughter, caused Prinny acute embarrassment. She strode manfully about, stood with legs apart and when she shook hands with any gentleman of the Court circles she nearly wrung off him arm. She probably behaved particularly badly in front of her father, sensing his irritation. Undoubtedly her aunts' and the Court ladies' praise of her father's exquisite manners must have made her own deliberately atrocious.

The Prince quarrelled with King George over the child's education, and poor girl, she must have had an unenviable time pulled between her grandparents, one of whom lost his wits, her portly father with his lax morals and unpredictable temper and her increasingly eccentric, high-spirited mother. She learnt to play one against the other, not surprisingly. Poor Charlotte was well aware that she dissimulated and wrote to a friend, in 1812, 'I have begun to *be false* also . . . it is the only thing here for defence, to use the same arms as they do'. She meant by 'they' the Prince Regent, his mother and his sisters, in this instance.

The quarrels between her father and her grandfather, not to mention those between her parents, who had separated before she was born, were not calculated to provide that stable, secure background which is believed to be so essential a start on which to build a well balanced and happy personality. Her grandfather felt

142

that his son was quite unfitted to the task of bringing up a future heir presumptive and indeed he would have liked the charge himself. His wife, Queen Charlotte, disliked her daughter-in-law as much as her son did, and was equally anxious to remove her grand-daughter from Caroline her mother.

Where she should live was a bone of contention. At first her home was in Carlton House or the next-door Warwick House with her father, her mother being allowed to see her periodically in the company of her governesses. Neither grandparent approved this arrangement, as they rightly suspected that the Prince, her father, was neglecting her. The Queen also wanted to get the little Princess away from her eccentric mother's influence. The eventual com-promise was that Charlotte lived with her father whenever he was in town, and when he was away she went to her grandparents at Windsor. Once a week she could see her mother, who very naturally kept up a constant war against this arrangement. As she was younger and gayer company than the ageing King and Queen, of course Charlotte preferred her company and the more amusing entourage of unconventional and free and easy friends. The régime at Windsor was stuffy and unbending, or, as Charlotte herself called it 'this den', 'this prison'.

So the little Princess grew up in comparative seclusion under the succession of governesses and tutors that were always in attendance on infant royalty. Till she was nine, the gay young governess called Miss Hayman assisted the Dowager Lady Elgin with her education. In 1797 this young woman wrote of her charge that she was 'the merriest little thing I ever saw—pepper-hot, too— if contradicted she kicks her little feet about in a great rage, but the cry ends in a laugh before you will know which it is'. Lady Elgin, writing just before she retired in 1805, says that her nine year old pupil was 'free from all fault whatever both in character and dis-position; that her mind was perfectly pure and innocent and that her progress in learning had been uncommonly sweet'. Whether she was a remarkably bad judge of character or whether she simply wished to please, her eulogy was far from the truth as the next governess-in-chief no doubt discovered. She was instructed that she must on no account let the Princess out of sight for a single instant, and keep her from her mother, both of which orders must have been impossible to execute.

Next, a 'lady-companion' was appointed to keep the Princess out of mischief, and Miss Cornelia Knight appeared on the scene. She was, the Princess afterwards said, 'an excellent valuable person, straightforward, open and honourable, clear-sighted and firm, accomplished and talented'. Finally this faithful friend was dismissed when she backed up Charlotte over her refusal to marry the Prince of Orange.

Poor Charlotte was for ever surrounded by spies and tale-bearers who were acting on behalf of one or other of her relations. It was hardly surprising that she was a difficult child to manage. However, she learnt drawing, music and French in a fairly slapdash way and in fact when she was only nine the King and Prince of Wales decided she should be largely taught by tutors.

The bad-tempered, pompous Dr Fisher was appointed chief tutor. A contemporary of Charlotte's, who knew the reverend doctor, wrote some years afterwards that 'he had no more knowledge of mankind than was to be acquired in the quadrangle of a college, where he had passed most of his life'. Charlotte herself referred to him as 'a bitter pill' though she had the sense 'never to give him cause for complaint or uneasiness'. Perhaps she thought the devil she knew was safer than a new devil. Dr Fisher was 57 years old and the lively, self-willed pupil found him, not unnaturally, 'tiresome and odious' when he taught her so solemnly and lectured her on her shortcomings.

A more successful tutor, for she had many instructors, was the Rev George Nott. He started his appointment with forebodings. He found Charlotte lazy, moody and bad-tempered; and a liar into the bargain. So exhausting did he find his wilful and emotional pupil that the poor man suffered a nervous breakdown. The Princess, as usual, was filled with remorse and wrote in May 1806, aged ten, 'I solemnly *declare* that I owe everything to Dr Nott . . . I must entreat the Almighty God . . . to forgive me my former sins and to implore the forgiveness of Dr Nott . . .'. Until, of course, the next fall from grace occurred. When Dr Nott returned she assured him he had never been out of her thoughts. She called herself his 'dutiful daughter by adoption'.

However, in 1809 Dr Nott's calvary came to an end, when some mischief-maker, probably the unlikeable Mrs Udney, accused Dr Nott of using influence over the Princess causing her to criticise her father and the under-governess, Mrs Udney. Nott, despite his protestations, was suspended and afterwards did very well both in the Church and in a literary career. Charlotte was devastated and wrote a letter in her best style, mourning his loss and promising to remember for ever his kindness and good advice.

Dr Short now took over, 'a good sort of Devonshire man', as Miss Cornelia Knight described him, adding that he had 'some classical knowledge, an honest heart, but over-cautious temper, fearful of offending'. He made it his business to brush up his pupil's English and he must have made himself acceptable as Charlotte kept him on as her chaplain after she married. Whether he did much to improve her spelling or tone down her delightfully racy, colourful language is another matter. In 1805 Dr Nott corrected over fifty spelling mistakes in the partly illegible six-page essay she did for him. In 1812 she was writing, 'Studdy is now my greatest resource, as it passes away hours of ennui'. She whiled away a good deal of time reading Byron, Mrs Edgeworth's romances, and, probably advised by her father who was an addict of Jane Austen's works, *Sense and Sensibility*. Perhaps the philosophical works of Diderot and *The Life and Campaign of Sir John Moore* were required reading from Dr Nott, but she also listed *The Sicilian Mysteries*, which sounds more exciting and wrote that she 'read a great deal both serious and light'. It was, after all, a period when people were accustomed to making their own amusements.

Charlotte liked to put on her green habit and the little straw hat and ride her small grey ponies round a large field at Bognor, seated in her 'chariot' beside her governess and driving over all the 'ruts and knolls and rugged places' so as to give her unfortunate companion a bit more exercise. She also enjoyed rambling along the beach and collecting berries which she would thread later into necklaces. She always enjoyed wild and tempestuous weather for these excursions. Looking after Charlotte can have been no bed of roses.

She was also very fond of fishing, but she always threw her catch back into the water after having tied a piece of ribbon round its tail.

The story of Charlotte's short life is poignant when we are forearmed with the knowledge of her early death, but of course she and her family luckily could not see into the future. The internecine warfare between her royal papa and eccentric mama caused her to write at one time, 'She is still my mother whether acting right or wrong and I cannot bear to think her unhappy'. At 16 she told her father furiously, when her mother had left the country, that Caroline had attempted to corrupt her daughter, leaving Captain Charles Hesse and herself locked in a bedroom with the words, 'à présent je vous laisse, amusez-vous'. Later she added cynically that she 'never could make out whether Capt Hesse was her lover (sic) or her mother's'. She certainly used the term in a platonic sense as far as she herself was concerned, but her father was sufficiently shaken to make her promise never to write to her mother again, nor to see her if ever she should return to England. To make sure, Charlotte was then, on Prinny's orders, compelled to write out a solemn document saying, 'I promise upon my honor (sic) never to write from this moment directly or indirectly to my mother and that all kind of communication shall cease and that I will abstain from seeing her when she comes to England'.

However, this promise made under duress did not prevent her from fleeing to her mother to get away from Slender Billy's unwelcome proposal of a Dutch alliance, which was advocated by the Prince Regent.

Caroline, who used to call her daughter 'my dear little Charlott . . . the dear little Angle', was as unreliable a port in a storm as ever the Prince Regent was. Poor Charlotte really had no safe haven to shelter her, though the aunts remained her devoted slaves. Sometimes she visited the Duchess of York at her home at Oatlands and was deafened by the yapping of the fifty pet dogs. Meanwhile her mother was constantly needling her father and grandparents about Charlotte's domicile, her education and general well-being, which drove Prinny, who himself was an arrant humbug, into passions of rage. Nothing is more unforgivable than your own faults mirrored in somebody else. He did not believe in Caroline's affectations of parental love, any more than she believed in his.

Once Charlotte was eighteen, in 1814, she was considered to be of age should she succeed to the throne. This was the occasion when all the eligible princes of Europe were ready to marry the future Queen of England. Prinny liked the idea of the Prince of Orange, but his daughter most certainly did not; partly because this unattractive young man, nick-named Slender Billy, first unwisely presented himself before her in a state of advanced intoxication to the young girl's considerable disgust. Secondly she spurned him because she had fallen headlong in love with Prince Augustus of Prussia, a young man of considerable experience with the fair sex. This fact did not come to light until 1949 when *Princess Charlotte's Letters* were published. As we have seen, the poor girl fled for help to that broken reed her unreliable, unbalanced mother. She could be assured of the admiration and support of the British populace at least and so could her mother, since Prinny had made himself extremely unpopular. But what Charlotte really needed was a kind, steady, dominating husband to take her in hand and give her security and love. This, by good fortune, she found in Leopold of Belgium, but the sad story of Princess Charlotte ended in 1817 when she was no longer a child and so does not concern us here. Everyone knows about the unhappy bungling of her dead baby's birth and her own untimely death. Leopold, her sorrowing husband, eventually became 'Uncle Leopold' to the young Queen Victoria, and that we shall hear about later.

When Sir Walter Scott, a great admirer as we have already seen of the little Scottish poetess 'Pet Marjory', was presented to the Duchess of Kent in 1828, he suspected that the little nine-year-old princess was well aware of her exalted position. The decree had, all the same, gone forth that she was to be given no hint of her probable inheritance of the throne of England, but how could she avoid overhearing the talk of her elders, who have the mistaken idea that children do not listen to what they are saying to one another.

Dignity was a natural gift which she was fortunate enough to be endowed with and the small, dumpy little figure always seems to have radiated a graciousness and majesty that many a handsomer person might have envied. Her German relatives called her 'the little English Mayflower', probably for the obvious reason that she was born in May. At home she was called by her first name, Alexandrina or Drina. As we know, her father, buoyed up by the gypsy's prophecy, never doubted but that she would come to the throne, often showing her to his friends saying, 'Look at her well, for she will be Queen of England'. As he died before his daughter was eight months old, this remark would not have penetrated her infant consciousness, of course. Her mother, however, was subsequently armed with the constant advice of her brother, Prince Leopold, whilst she brought up her fatherless child. Uncle Leopold, the sorrowing widower of Princess Charlotte who died in 1817, was able to be a forceful influence by correspondence in the life of his niece, even though he himself had been thwarted from becoming King of England. If he was authoritarian, his sister was equally severe, and there must have been many battles between the disciplinarian mother and her self-willed little daughter, who particularly disliked the word 'must' when it was addressed to herself. Uncle Leopold of Saxe-Coburg was elected King of the Belgians in 1831. He married Marie-Louise d'Orleans, daughter of Louis-Philippe, very diplomatically, and had a son in 1835. It was his nephew Albert, born in 1819, who became Prince Consort, a position which Leopold might have held had Princess Charlotte lived.

Was it Uncle Leopold's idea that Victoria should breakfast frugally on bread-and-milk and fruit at 8 o'clock every day? She protested tearfully that she wanted Mama's sausages and her governess's caraway seeds; but in vain. After breakfast she went out for a walk or a drive, lasting about an hour. Then her mother taught her from 10 o'clock until 12 o'clock so that by four years old she could write her name very creditably. At 2 o'clock they had luncheon,

147

Staffordshire figures of Queen Victoria and Prince Albert, probably with their first baby, the Princess Royal. Photograph by Jennifer May.

which was also a very simple affair, and this was followed by lessons again until 4 o'clock, after which there was another walk or a drive or perhaps a visit. At dinner the little princess sat by her mother and was allowed to have dessert, presumably having watched the Duchess enjoy a good hearty meal. At 9 o'clock she was packed off to the bed which was beside that of her mother. Probably Victoria was brought up on that household Bible of the late eighteenth and early nineteenth century homes, *Domestic Medicine* by Dr William Buchan. He was a strong believer in plain fare. Bread-and-milk for breakfast and for supper, 'enriched with fruits, sugar and such things', was his recommendation. He was of a very pessimistic nature, remarking, 'miserable indeed is the lot of man in the state of infancy'. However, to his credit he prescribed many more vegetables in the diet than had been used before, advising that children be given mutton and potatoes, carrots, turnips, salsify, beets, onions and leeks. Moreover, he encouraged walking in the fresh air with gardening, fieldwork and dancing for children, though he seems to have regarded cheese with suspicion.

What Victoria enjoyed most was to run about in Kensington Gardens or to be drawn in her little carriage by the donkey. Then she could hold out her hand to her future loyal subjects who hastened to kiss it and to cheer her.

By the time she was twelve, Victoria spoke French and German and was 'acquainted with Italian'. She had also been taught Latin and Greek, Mathematics, Music and Drawing. Her schoolroom books included the redoubtable Mrs Trimmer's *History of England* and *Roman History*. As the Trimmers, mother and daughter, were so adamant about the ill-effects of fairy-tales, the little princess was probably not stimulated imaginatively by those delightful stories of Charles Perrault, like *Beauty and the Beast, Cinderella* and other famous tales. Victoria was passionately fond of riding, danced well and excelled in archery, however, so life was not all hard work.

When she was eleven she was told about how near she was to the throne, but goodness knows she must have been remarkably stupid if she had not guessed this truth by then; Victoria was *not* stupid. She dutifully vowed repeatedly, 'I will be good' and this excellent maxim was approvingly noticed by her family.

The princess's nursery at Kensington Palace was the prototype of all the nurseries of the period. Some of the delightful toys she played with can be seen in the London Museum. The rather austere, humble little dolls' house, and some of the 132 German pegwooden dolls which she dressed with the help of her governess, Baroness Lehzen, are there, for instance. Generally speaking, the first quarter of the nineteenth century was a very spartan time for nurseries. Charlotte Yonge's 'passage room' was not exceptional. The discipline of most nurseries was firm but kind, with the nurse all-powerful, the parents remote but kind and the children wrapped in a reassuring sense of security and safety, whether they were royal or whether they were children 'whose dear Papa was poor'.

Inspired by the Evangelical and Oxford Movements, children were supplied with hard chairs and plain food. Parents, governesses and nurses were all decidedly strict by our standards. Tears and tribulation were preferred to temptations and sinful delights. The austerities of Sundays were particularly depressing, more especially in Scotland. What with having to learn the Collect and some hymns and as likely as not long and probably incomprehensible excerpts from the Bible, the children were given little time for anything more light-hearted. Church, with a long sermon and probably the Litany into the bargain, must have made a very bleak day for the younger generation. A Presbyterian child would have had to answer the question, 'What is man's chief end'? by replying, 'To glorify God and enjoy Him for ever'. One might have been forgiven for wondering where the enjoyment came in, with the prospect of so much of

Puzzle picture of Queen Victoria, the Prince Consort and their first two children, the Princess Royal and the Prince of Wales. Photograph by Studio Wreford.

'God's wrath and curse' and only the dimmest possibility of reaching the Elysian Fields and the bliss there to be expected.

However, in Kensington Palace the little Princess Victoria, described by Harriet, Countess Granville as 'le roi Georges in petticoats' lived a secluded life and hardly ever seems to have seen the Royal Family. When she thought of Uncle this always meant Uncle Leopold. Her governess, Baroness Lehzen, had looked after the Duchess of Kent's daughter by her first marriage and took on little Victoria at the age of five, staying on with her till she was 18.

Creevey, rather unfairly, called the Duchess of Kent, 'the most restless, persevering, troublesome devil possible'. Certainly Victoria had many a painful episode with her mother during her teens, but one of her qualities was intense loyalty and even much later on in her life she never seems to have alluded to this difficult period. Sir John Conroy and Lady Flora Hastings tried to establish in the minds of her entourage that she was too stupid to reign without a Regent should she become Queen at eighteen, when she would be of age. Luckily Stockman, Melbourne and Baroness Lehzen were at hand to champion, to guide and to protect her.

The princess was only 4 feet 10 inches tall when fully grown, but her small plump figure and high colour was, as we have already emphasised, balanced by an immense dignity of manner. True, she had a quick temper and was both self-willed and obstinate, but she never bore malice and she was exceedingly affectionate.

By 1841 her own children were beginning to fill the nursery, so now we will take a look at one of them in particular. In November 1841 the Queen mentioned the birth of the Prince of Wales in her Journal, significantly adding, 'Albert brought in dearest little Pussy (the Princess Royal) in such a smart white meriono dress . . . and placed her on my bed, seating himself next to her, and she was very dear and good'. She always adored this first child and later 'Puss' became Empress of Germany.

ALBERT EDWARD, PRINCE OF WALES
1841–1910

In his mother's published letters, her sharp and often thoroughly unpleasant criticisms of her children, particularly of the Prince of Wales later on in his life, are only too well known. The reason for these disapproving comments appears to be that the Prince Consort believed that it was better to express disapproval on paper. This was presumably on the assumption that tempers would then have cooled and the written word can be pruned and softened. The disadvantage of this method, especially when the family is a royal one, is obvious. Letters are kept and read by posterity. Family quarrels could have passed into blessed oblivion, perhaps, but written down they are given the full glare of publicity and consequently a legend is born. The belief that Queen Victoria disliked her eldest son and was negligent of her children is now a firmly held opinion. Yet, when she was dying, she breathed the pet-name of the Prince of Wales, and not that of her adored husband.

In such a large family of five girls and four boys it is asking too much of human nature to expect the parents to avoid having favourites. When the eldest child was nearly seventeen the youngest was born and four years later their father died at the age of forty-two. The Prince of Wales was then twenty. The elder children always suspected the youngest were preferred.

Like many other distinguished people of his age,* Edward was a tiny child. He was very fair, with his mother's high colour and he seems to have been a great chatterbox. His outspokenness was quite a trial to his parents. Like his mother, he too was very affec-tionate, loving people rather than things. He developed into an easy-going, charming companion. When he grew up his manners were said to be impeccable. Tact, judgment, affability and dignity were the adjectives used when describing the Prince in his maturity.

For the first seven years of his life he was looked after by his mother's Lady of the Bedchamber, Lady Lyttelton, when, if we are to believe the contemporary accounts, he was a little angel of goodness, already possessing beautiful manners and making great use of those prominent blue eyes which he had inherited from his mother. Lady Lyttelton was a sister of Mrs Gladstone.

Reporters and gossips had no access to the royal nurseries as both the Queen and Prince Albert were determined that the children should be sheltered from the 'fierce light' which sooner or later is bound to be directed upon royalty. Osborne perhaps gives the most vivid picture of the home life of Queen Victoria's family, as we shall see presently.

When the young Queen Victoria came to the throne at 18 years old, the Lord Chamberlain was responsible for lighting fires, but their laying was in the department of the Lord Steward, who also ordered the cleaning and lighting of all the lamps, which were sup-plied by the Lord Chamberlain. His department saw to the cleaning of the royal windows inside; but the Master of the Woods and Forests had the job of cleaning the outside. The Lord Chamberlain

*Louis-Philippe, Franz Joseph, *et al.*

looked after forty housemaids at Buckingham Palace and forty housemaids at Windsor, whilst cooks were under the dominion of the Lord Steward and footmen belonged to the Master of the Horse.

It sounds a chaotic arrangement and when Prince Albert came on the scene he did not take long to look into these domestic affairs with a reforming eye. He cut down staff, reduced wages and improved sanitation. Finally, combining the highest offices of the establishment into one comprehensive whole, he created the Master of the Royal Household to oversee all these matters. This, of course, meant a handsome saving to the Queen's privy purse.

By 1845 they had economised sufficiently to buy the estate of Osborne on the Isle of Wight. Here they built a new house 'in the Italianate style' and here they made a typically Victorian family home with a typically Victorian collection of objects which they both loved. It is said that there were over 2,000 small objects of bric-à-brac in Osborne by the end of Victoria's reign. The children, frozen into Parian or marble images, remained ever young. Every room and corridor and alcove was full of *bibelots* of all sorts. The new art of daguerreotype was much in evidence, portraying the Royal Family in all their great variety and the children at various ages and in various disguises too, as they were fond of acting in plays or charades.

Miss Mary Thornycroft was one of the many sculptors pressed into service; and she was responsible for the macabre case of life-sized feet, legs, arms and hands in marble which are displayed on black velvet at Osborne. She also modelled the royal children in marble as the Four Seasons and Peace and Plenty. Her imagination rather lost impetus by the end of the series and she portrayed Prince Leopold simply as a 'fisher-boy' and the baby Princess Beatrice is bashfully nestling in a sea-shell. Their father, by the way, kept two of the marble limbs in his dressing-room beside his shaving mirror, a great tribute to Miss Thornycroft's art, she must have felt. The Prince also liked frescoes. Some were instructive, some uplifting and some allegorical. Oh, dear! They were all huge and Albert's own favourite was in his dressing-room, an enormous figure of Neptune and some lesser gods handing over the Empire of the sea to Britannia. Does that strike a nostalgic note? His bathroom enshrines, rather strangely, the marriage of Hercules and Omphale. Well, perhaps the Achilles' heel of the royal pair was their lack of humour.

Never let it be forgotten, however, that Albert was a man of brilliant gifts and he seems to have been interested in everything

153

from the arts to mining and industry; witness the two chairs at Osborne sculpted out of coal and those repulsive and miserably uncomfortable ones with legs made of stags' antlers. Whoever dreamed up that idea?

The 'Horn Room' featured other pieces of furniture made from the antlers of deer and the table tops were inlaid with deer horn. Another oddity, rather more appealing than all those enshrined memorials of stag-hunting, was the picture of the original old Osborne House portrayed entirely from the coloured sands of Alum Bay.

As for the pictures, these ranged from porcelain plaques painted with views to colossal works by Landseer and by Winterhalter, the Court painter. Albert's own collection of German castles and his splendid Italian primitives are now no longer at Osborne. They must have been rather strange bedfellows with the pictures Victoria commissioned from Landseer of Princess Victoria's macaw and 'some trusted ghillies and keepers'. These last were, of course, in honour of Scotland and besides all this *embarras de richesses* there were innumerable statuettes and portraits and lots and lots of dogs. Had not *The Times* called Landseer 'The Shakespeare of dogs'? In particular the Queen had ordered marble portraits of her collie dog called, with some reason, Sharp, and another bad-tempered collie dog called, less appropriately perhaps, Noble. The Queen's horse only rated plaster.

Nevertheless, what a delightful place this homely palace must have seemed to the royal children. Except for a noticeable stern harshness of manner towards the Prince of Wales, Albert seems to have been the ideal father, cherishing them, singing to them and caressing them. He it was who designed a child-size Swiss chalet in the grounds of Osborne and a miniature kitchen for the little princesses to practise their baking and cookery. Moreover, the results of their labours were often produced at the tea-table and heroically sampled by their parents. There was also a splendid carpentry shop for the princess and that fort-shaped musical-box, the pride and joy of Albert as it played *con brio* a chorus from *Tannhäuser*, would have delighted the children too. Were they ever allowed to tinkle on their mother's 'personal piano'? It was a huge square one, heavily inlaid and gilded and it stood massively on plump legs which looked like outsize sticks of barley sugar. (Do children nowadays ever get that appetising sweet, I wonder?) The State drawing-room piano is far too grand for even royal children to play. It is inlaid with porcelain plaques and encrusted with ormolu.

By 1855 a new home was opened in Scotland. This 'dear Paradise', as the Queen called it, adding that it was 'my dear Albert's own creation' was to be even more of a beloved home than Osborne. Balmoral Castle built in Scottish baronial style was entirely to Prince Albert's taste and his fond wife was delighted to live in this memorial to his 'great taste' where the 'impress of his dear hand had been stamped everywhere'. Here were to be found more Parian Highlanders holding up lights, an overpowering display of wall-papers with gold thistles on a blue background, upholstery and curtains predominantly in Royal Stuart tartan, hunting Stuart and dress Stuart. More thistles adorned some of the chintzes. Colourful it certainly was, but a lady-in-waiting voiced her own reservations in muted sentences referring mildly to 'a certain absence of harmony of the whole . . . all highly characteristic and appropriate, but not equally *flatteux* (sic) to the eye'.

To the royal pair, however, it was Elysium, or at least Victoria found it so. Whether the highly intellectual and serious-minded Albert found the simple jokes and gossip favoured by the Queen even bearable is questionable. Those endless evenings when the gentlemen joined the ladies and looked at family photograph albums, tinkled on the piano or chatted about the trivia of the day must have been martyrdom to Albert, longing as he did for intelligent mascu-line conversation about philosophy and science, books, world affairs and academic matters. Unfortunately the Queen did not even welcome reading out loud, which Albert would have been very glad to have provided whilst the ladies were occupied with their crochet or needlework or tatting. They at least had music in com-mon and sang together of an evening and entertained musicians such as Mendelssohn with great mutual satisfaction.

The habit of eating chocolate came in during the early years of Victoria's reign. Cadbury advertised 'French Eating Chocolate' in 1842. One can therefore be permitted to imagine this delicious con-fection being eaten in the royal nurseries. Up till now chocolate was only used as a drink. The royal children must have needed com-pensations for their mother's coldness to them. Her extremely pas-sionate nature, a legacy from her 'wicked uncles' seems to have been balanced by her complete and self-confessed lack of interest in the children. '. . . I find no special pleasure or compensation in the company of the elder children', she wrote in 1856. 'Only very ex-ceptionally do I find the rather intimate intercourse with them either agreeable or easy'. No wonder that the Prince of Wales, at 50, blanched with fear before entering the august presence of his for-midable mother. In 1862 Lady Clarendon, wife of the Foreign Secretary, wrote in her diary, '. . . the serious misfortune Lord

Palmerston sees looking ahead is her (the Queen's) unconquerable aversion to the Prince of Wales'. Later she continues, 'She got quite excited when speaking of him (Edward) and said it quite irritated her to see him in the room. I believe the poor boy knows of his mother's dislike of him, but seems to have the good taste not to speak of it'.

It does certainly look as if the Queen was unfair to her son. Albert, speaking confidentially to Lord Clarendon, does admit to his concern about the royal children's education and the Queen's 'aggressive' system. The significant remark he made to the Foreign Secretary about 'the alarm he felt lest the Queen's mind should be excited by any opposition to her will' recalls the ever-present fear for the Queen's sanity, which she seems to have often used as a threat. Stockmar noted that Prince Albert lived 'in perpetual terror of bringing on the hereditary malady'. Poor man, the disagreeable task of punishing his children for their offences generally devolved upon him. Though this may seem fair enough, it must have been irksome sometimes to punish them for sins he did not feel were very heinous. While not contesting the truth of all these criticisms of Queen Victoria, and those mentioned here are but the visible part of the iceberg, it is worth remembering again what a goldfish bowl famous people live in. Moreover, the public is much more interested in foibles than in virtues, and so are most diarists and letter-writers.

Prince Edward of Wales cannot have had an easy childhood, but there were many compensations. One of the sailors on the Royal Yacht had a copy of a man-of-war suit made for the Prince. Winterhalter made a charming portrait of him when he was seven years old, wearing his sailor-suit, and this probably started a fashion for the garment, both for boys and girls, which went on from 1850 until the end of the century. In fact, so popular was the sailor-suit that when he was himself a parent Edward dressed his own little boys in the same style.

Prince Edward learnt to appreciate France as early as 1855 when he was 14 and joined his parents and his elder sister, the Princess Royal, in a visit to the Emperor Napoleon III and the Empress Eugénie. The visit was all too short for the little Prince who begged that he and his sister be allowed to stay on. When the Empress tactfully suggested that his mother would not like to be parted from her two oldest children he cried, 'Not do without us! Don't fancy that, for there are six more of us at home, and they don't want *us*'. One feels this may well have been one of the occasions when the Queen was not amused.

After the Archbishop of Canterbury had exhaustively examined him for an hour at his Confirmation, the Prince went on a short holiday to Ireland and then returned to the White Lodge, Richmond, where he and his tutor and governor were joined by three young chosen companions. The following year, in 1859, he set off with the tutor on a long tour of the Continent, foreign travel being considered to be the best possible education for a Prince. So he visited Rome and stayed there quite a long time and afterwards went on to Gibralter and Lisbon. Summing up his childhood, we have a picture of elderly tutors struggling to teach a distinctly reluctant pupil mathematics, geology, political economy and history and many other subjects, and visitors to entertain the young Prince at Windsor such as carefully chosen Eton boys, who noted later that the Prince's papa cast a considerable blight over the 'play' times. He 'inspired a feeling of dread' was the verdict. Certainly Albert preferred his son to consort with 'serious men of advanced years'. One university was not enough, either. Edinburgh, Oxford and Cambridge all received His Royal Highness. On the credit side, he seems to have emerged virtually unscathed from his terrifying curricula, as everyone mentioned his good nature, his cheerfulness, his ease of manner, his charming smile and his interest in people.

Yes, there certainly were compensations in his childhood to make up for any undue severity from his parents. It was much later on that he felt the strain, when he was grown-up and married with children of his own and yet still under the formidable thumb of his tiny, plump, rheumatic, but exceedingly regal mama, always dressed in black in honour of Albert and ever conscious of her position as a ruler over 398 million subjects; it cannot have been his childhood which irked the future King Edward VII nearly so much as its prolongation into his adult life. Queen Victoria died in 1902, when the heir to the throne was over 60.

CHAPTER EIGHT

The Grand Tour

Richard Lassels was one of the first of a long line of 'Governors' who subsequently made quite a profession of taking young Englishmen from families rich enough to afford it, across Europe to complete their education. He was born in Lincolnshire in 1603, the year James I came to the throne, but by 1629 he was teaching Classics at the Catholic exiles' College at Douai. From there he started his 'three long voyages into Flanders, six into France, five into Italy, one into Germany and Holland', acting as 'bear-leader', which was the popular name given to these invaluable tutors of the young nobility. Lassels believed Italy should be the Mecca for these tours. He preferred young gentlemen of fifteen or sixteen and he advised parents that in Italy their son could 'season his mind with the gravity and wise maxims of that nation which has civilised the whole world'. Some boys, nevertheless, went abroad at fourteen or even eleven, like Robert Boyle, the youngest son of the Earl of Cork's family of fourteen children. In fact Grand Tours had been the fashion as early as 1572 when Sir Philip Sidney went on one at the age of eighteen. He was then only Mr Philip Sidney and travelled with the Lord High Admiral and an older companion to the Paris of Charles IX. By the end of the eighteenth century the trickle of travellers had grown to a positive river. It was not always an unqualified success. One young nobleman of seventeen went to Rome and by a year later he had gambled away about £3,000.

Other nationalities sent boys on these tours, but perhaps to a lesser degree. We shall meet a French boy later on who spent several months in England very profitably. Boswell went on a tour, but poor Dr Johnson never visited Italy and felt a strong and lasting sense of inferiority in consequence. In his day it had become a real status symbol to be able to boast of continental travel.

A tour in the eighteenth century must have been quite a test of endurance, what with the dangers from bandits, the grasping stage-coach drivers, cheating innkeepers and hazards of passing over the Alps. It comes as something of a surprise to learn that passports were necessary. We find John Evelyn having to produce one at Antwerp, and he obtained one of 'extraordinary length and magnificence' when he went from Padua to Milan, which was then under the dominion of Spain. Boswell, when he went to Corsica, had to provide himself with one and even more tiresomely travellers had to produce health certificates. As for money, that was another complication. Travellers bills of exchange were sent to the required foreign city to be collected at a suitable rate settled on by the merchant bankers. More conveniently, our own English banks took over when they were started at the end of the seventeenth century. In the eighteenth century it must have been quite a nightmare changing currencies at every little frontier in Italy and Germany where there were so many separate principalities.

Another burden was the familiar one of tipping, but it was then far worse than nowadays. A positive army of servants lines up for their 'vails' even if the traveller only stopped for half-an-hour at an acquaintance's home and nobody offered him so much as a drink.

The young noblemen on their tours were obliged to provide themselves with every kind of necessity. A lady writing at the end of the eighteenth century advised travellers to equip themselves with bedclothes, ample provisions of sugar, tea, pepper and mustard, oatmeal and soup, and on no account to omit a good selection of medicines. They were also strongly recommended to take along a really good door bolt. One might with advantage make use of a sort of Cook's tour guide called a *vetturino* or *voiturin*. This convenient traveller's aid would be prepared to arrange transport, lodgings, meals and freedom from bandits at a fixed lump sum. To be sure he might be a mixed blessing. The billeting of strangers in your bedroom or even your bed might be the least of your troubles.

Arrival on the shores of England again presented more problems. The customs officers were not easy to outface and even Horace Walpole had a story to tell about having to pay duty to the tune of seven-and-a-half guineas on a miserable 'set of coffee things that had cost me but five'.

MASTER COKE OF NORFOLK AND SOME OTHERS

When Thomas Coke of Norfolk was fifteen he was the fortunate possessor of an income of about £10,000 a year. Other contemporaries were living in comparative comfort on considerably less. Parson Woodforde, for example, did very well on his £300 a year, paying two maids to look after him, a footman, a boy for the rough jobs in the house and a farm labourer. He gave them, besides their keep, £30 12s a year between them.

Thomas Coke was therefore very rich indeed and he needed to be to go on a Grand Tour in proper state. Indeed when William Beckford went across Europe with his retinue he was once mistaken for the Russian Emperor. Thomas Coke became an orphan at the age of ten and was at first quite unaware of his worldly wealth. His guardians sent him to a boarding-school, where he seems to have stayed in the holidays as well, being cared for by a tutor and no less than five personal servants. When he was removed at the age of fourteen to a relative's home on account of ill health he recovered quickly and began to sow his wild oats, drinking with unsuitable neighbours, becoming too familiar with the servants and spending his days hunting instead of doing his lessons. Foreign travel seemed the best way to deal with the spirited and unruly boy, so off he went in 1712 with a 'governor' called Dr Thomas Hobart. They also took along a steward to look after their arrangements and keep accounts. His name was Edward Jarrett. This invaluable man later became Coke's house-steward when, at the age of twenty-one he married and set up house in Bloomsbury. Incidentally, the staff numbered 30 souls looking after the two Cokes.

Sensibly enough they started the tour in Paris and Versailles and then Hobart took his young charge to the Loire valley to enter 'an academy for gentlemanly accomplishments'. Certainly the fogs at Blois were not much to their liking but they had the enjoyment of a lot of English society there. Moreover at Angers, when they went there, they found the company of 'young bloods', much to Thomas's pleasure, whose heads were full of hounds and horses but nothing very much more. Young Thomas Coke was, however, an intellectual in the making, though he certainly enjoyed all the usual pursuits of his age as well. In fact the two sides of his nature were often at war; but by the time he had gone on a tour of six months all over France and visited the opera and taken music lessons, learning to play the trumpet, the flute and the flageolet, he was turning into quite a nice balance of good brains and good sportsmanship, even if he did object to discipline and became more and more aware of the handsome future he was to inherit. After the French tour an extensive tour of Italy followed and he mixed learning with some masquerades and visits to the opera. Thomas was not only learning Italian now, but also being instructed in architecture. Neither Thomas Coke nor William Kent, when they met in Naples, realised that 'the father of modern gardening' had found his future patron.

Thomas was by now so delighted with the culture of Italy that he began a colossal buying spree. He acquired pictures, busts and bas-reliefs, rare manuscripts and editions of magnificent books.

160

One purchase included no less than the whole section of a monastery library comprised of works none of which was later than the fifteenth century. His popularity amongst the Italians was consequently assured. Most of his collection was shipped back home and already he was planning to rebuild his home, Holkham Hall, and to furnish it with this great collection of works of art.

On he went next to Vienna, but this he found 'a very dull place'. The Court ladies seem to have been unattractively stout and he consoled himself gambling and playing his flute. The next stop was Dresden, where some English noblemen of his own age took him to see Hanover, The Hague, Amsterdam and Brussels.

Though not realising it till much later, Richard Boyle, Earl of Burlington was travelling at the same time over much the same ground, he having come into his inheritance at the age of ten. He was three years older than Coke. He had possessions in Ireland and in Yorkshire, not to mention a lot of land in London north of Piccadilly, including Burlington House. He it was who owned Chiswick House, which he ordered to be built in 1725, having been inspired whilst on his tour by Palladio's Villa Capra. William Kent was engaged to decorate the rooms. He started his tour in the Low Countries and his entourage consisted of a tutor and several servants as well as gentlemen of taste and culture to stimulate his interests in the Arts of the Continent. He too bought innumerable treasures during his journeys, including a couple of harpsichords and a bass viol, a great many pictures, *objets d'art* of all kinds and the inevitable vases that travellers always brought back. To keep him company a positive retinue of dogs, increased by one called Dye who was given a special basket bought in Rome for her 'to pup in', as well as a quilt and a great deal of milk. He spent a year travelling and eventually reached Dover with no less than 878 pieces of baggage to get through the Customs. Nor surprisingly the officers were not very pleased with the young milord, but were very easily appeased by the remarkably small tip of half a guinea.

Taking dogs abroad seems to have been quite common. Horace Walpole on his tour, taken at the age of twenty-one with Thomas Gray and Richard West in 1739, also had a dog with him when crossing the Alps. It was a little black King Charles's spaniel called Tory and 'the prettiest, fattest, dearest creature'. Alas, it suffered a dreadful fate that upset its master very much indeed. He tells the story in a letter: 'I had let it out of the chaise for the air and it was waddling along close to the head of the horses . . . by the side of a wood of firs. There darted out a young wolf, seized poor dear Tory by the throat and before we could possibly prevent it, sprung up

161

Punch looks at the influence of tours abroad on English food habits. The drawing is by John Leech. Photograph by Studio Wreford.

the side of the rock and carried him off'. He ends the account, 'It was shocking to see anyone one loved run away with to so horrid a death'. Whether he was then wearing the fashionable Parisian waistcoat and tight breeches, lace ruffles and muff which he bought in Paris we don't know. He had not much enjoyed his first visit to France, not yet speaking the language fluently enough to benefit from the intellectual salons that would have suited his tastes. In fact at the opera he found the music unacceptable and later he remarked, 'if we did not remember there was such a place as England, we should know nothing about it: the French never mention it, unless it happens to be in one of their proverbs!' Nor did the weather help. He therefore took a jaundiced look at 'Versailles le Grand' in the rain and then they went on to Rheims where he fared no better. Walpole enjoyed the company of friends more than he enjoyed sight-seeing. In Florence, although welcomed hospitably by the *Chargé d'affaires* Horace Mann, Walpole was no better pleased at all the paintings and architecture than he had been in France. 'I see several things that please me calmly', he admitted, 'but I have left off screaming Lord! this! and Lord! that!' Once the carnival season began he was happier, and took part gaily in all the masked parties to the Opera and balls, patronising the coffee houses and shops. The only sights in Italy he was really pleased with were the antiquities of Herculaneum. Pompeii was not discovered till 1763, eight years after Walpole's travels.

The years from 1763 to the outbreak of the French Revolution in 1793 saw the peak of the successful Tours. After this their educational value began to degenerate into something of a social necessity for the upper classes, a sort of status symbol. More and more young men went abroad and came back much as they started with little to show for the expensive 'finishing' but a smattering of French, Italian and German, and not always even that. Probably the French Revolution followed by the Napoleonic Wars spelled the end of the Grand Tour in its old style.

Tourists now began to flood the Continent and in 1808 the significant birth took place in Derbyshire of Thomas Cook, the future pioneer of organised travel holidays for the masses. He left school at ten, worked as a wood-turner first and then became an itinerant Baptist preacher at twenty successfully, due to his fine presence and flashing eyes. He married and his son, who was later his partner, was born and named John Mason Cook. After several years organising excursion trains, which he pioneered, offering cheap fares for special occasions, this enterprising man ran tours to visit the 1851 Exhibition and the Paris Exhibition of 1855. In 1867 tourists galore visited the mammoth 1867 French Exhibition. Cook and his son went from strength to strength and so travel agents replaced the 'governors' and *vetturinos* and the pattern of travel was completely transformed.

Now everybody, or nearly everybody, could travel abroad and they went to enjoy themselves and laugh at the oddities of the foreigner, whereas in the eighteenth century and earlier travel was

M

undertaken primarily to broaden the horizons of the educated minority and encourage them to lap up the arts and bring back as many pictures, sculpture and bibelots as they could afford to enrich the stately homes of England. Indeed we might say that when Thomas Cook started his circular pleasure tours in the 1840s here was the landmark where privilege in travel ended and the age of Mr Everyman the tourist began.

Young women, quite obviously, never made the Grand Tour as their education was certainly not geared towards foreign travel. The few who managed such adventurous holidays were either married, like Lady Fetherstonhaugh who travelled for two years in 1749 on a protracted and enjoyable honeymoon; or they were no longer young and therefore do not come into our story.

A YOUNG FRENCHMAN IN ENGLAND
1784

Seeing ourselves as others see us is a valuable insight and the memoirs of young François de la Rochefoucauld when he was travelling in England in 1784 gives a delightful glimpse of eighteenth century life in the country between Plymouth, Liverpool and Bury St Edmunds. Fashionable Frenchmen made a point of cultivating *anglomanie* at this period and it is interesting to see England from the viewpoint of a young man of nineteen making his Grand Tour. François's father, the duc de Lioncourt, Louis XVI's Master of the Wardrobe, entered his son in the army as a gentleman-cadet and he became sub-lieutenant by the age of sixteen. Then he completed his education by travelling round France, followed by a tour in England to learn the language and culture. He travelled with his younger brother and a Polish companion called Maximilien de Lazowski to guide them. They also took their French servants with them. The first part of their stay was at Bury St Edmunds so as to be near their father's friend Arthur Young who was the first authority on agriculture in England and the celebrated author of *Annals of Agriculture*. He was interested in more than farming; he could talk with enthusiasm and knowledge of the arts in general, politics and trade. This of course explains the friendship between the Rochefoucaulds *père et fils* and Young. The duc de Lioncourt was also a highly cultivated man, his chief interests, however, being agriculture and industry. What is of interest to us in our context of Grand Tours is the general observations of François on English ways of life. He kept a careful and comprehensive travel diary for the benefit of his father.

François' first comment on reaching England was upon the inconvenience of a coal fire compared with a log fire. His earliest experience of this phenomenon was on his arrival at Dover in bitterly cold January weather. However, he learnt after some time in heavy snow and frost to prefer the additional warmth thrown out by coal, even if it smelt so disagreeable.

Once in London they settled in King Street, St James's, the fashionable quarter of town, and admired the shops which were so clean and so chock-full of excellent merchandise. He obliged his father with a good deal of historical background, which we will skip here, and discuss rather his sketches of the Englishman's day in London. There is, he notes, little time for work. He rises at about ten and has breakfast with tea; tours the town till 5 o'clock which is dinner time; at 9 o'clock he meets his friends in a club or a tavern and there spends the rest of the evening in drinking and gambling. No, not much time for work indeed. The women are all at home with their children, meanwhile, whilst their husbands arc ruining the family gambling to such high stakes. François found the educated man's way of spending their days eating and drinking together very strange.

From London the party went to Bury, in Suffolk, and here François suffered the indignity of being followed by people who had never seen any Frenchmen before, jeering, 'Frenchies, Frenchies'. He did not enjoy visiting Arthur Young much, although he enjoyed his company. 'His table', complains the young man, 'is the worst and dirtiest possible and . . . his wife . . . looks exactly like a devil. She continually torments her children and her servants and is most frequently ill-tempered towards her visitors'.

The total consumption of tea amazed young François, 'The humblest peasant has his tea twice a day just like a rich man,' he noticed, amounting to at least four pounds of tea per person per year. When they weren't drinking tea they were swigging down cider and beer. He noticed that the English employed more servants than the French, mostly in the kitchen and stables. In the house they worked to a high standard of cleanliness, every Saturday washing the whole house from attic to basement 'outside and in'. Yet, François goes on to say, English servants are 'the laziest set of people it is possible to meet'. Apparently he means the valets, who simply waited at table and dressed their masters' hair. Later on he found that the cleanliness in English houses was only skin-deep. 'I need only mention the kitchen—the dirt is indescribable'. As for the women employed there they are 'black as coal; their arms, bared to the elbow, are disgustingly dirty; to save time they handle the portions of food with their hands'. Were French kitchens better? The inference is that they most certainly were.

Spending the day with a Duke or with a Squire the formula was always the same. Breakfast about 9 o'clock in company and everybody dressed for the day. In France of course breakfast was always a private meal before leaving the bedroom, so nobody would have been wearing anything but a *robe-de-chambre*. Breakfast consisted of tea and sometimes coffee and chocolate, with bread and butter and the morning papers to stifle conversation. It was a very unsociable occasion and the men could wear riding-boots and a shabby coat, and nobody took much notice of anybody else.

However, the standard of behaviour, reports François, is 'uncomfortably high', and rigid with etiquette by the evening. Two full hours spent in the actual eating of dinner are followed by the servants' departure once they have removed the table cloth and set upon the brilliantly polished mahogany all kinds of wines, some fruit and 'biscuits to stimulate thirst'. The ladies take a glass or two and then leave and after this 'the real enjoyment begins'. Free conversation and endless drinking of toasts continues for two or three hours and then a servant announces that tea is served in the drawing-room and the inebriated men join the ladies in tea-drinking and playing whist till midnight. Cold meat is provided for the starving guests. All this time punch is ready on a side-table for anyone who wants still more to drink. What a physical ordeal it sounds. At least in the country they broke up at 10 o'clock, but of course dinner began earlier, about 3 o'clock, so the ordeal by eating and drinking was not much shorter, and into the bargain the invited guests had to get themselves home over the bumpy roads. In spite of the etiquette imposed before dining François told his father delightedly, 'It would be impossible to be more easy-going in good society than one is in England'. The young people of his age, for instance, particularly the girls, were very informal not to say 'lacking in polite behaviour' compared with his friends in France. They never received any instruction in manners. He describes how they 'hum under their breath, they whistle, they sit down in a large armchair and put their feet on another, they sit on any table in the room and do a thousand things which would be ridiculous in France'. Is there a note of envy in his words, as he tells his father about this permissive society? He admits that they might not be quite so free and easy in London society, but certainly at home they behave like this amongst their friends. Later he explains that in England the words happiness and liberty are practically synonymous.

As for husbands and wives, the young Frenchman was surprised to find that they were 'always together, sharing the same society. It is the rarest thing to meet the one without the other'. Food for thought is here, implying that French husbands and wives seldom were in each other's company. In fact young François admits that seeing these happy couples he is inclined to feel an English wife would suit him better than a French one.

In England, he reports, 'the young folk are in society from an early age; they go with their parents everywhere. Young girls mix with the company and talk and enjoy themselves with as much freedom as if they were married'. He adds that 'three marriages out of four are based on affection'. He informs us that 30 years before, that is in the 1750s, 'the first man in sight could marry a pair', and no priest was needed, a practice still holding good (in 1784) in Scotland; nor was parental consent required for a marriage. François did not approve, so he assures his father, of Gretna Green runaway marriages which flouted authority, for 'whom can we respect if not our parents?' He was equally surprised to learn that English couples took a house and lived alone in it, avoiding living even in the same town as the parents. Whereas in France the whole family with their wives and children lived, if not in the same house, certainly in the same neighbourhood. 'Marriage before the age of 25 or 28 is rare', remarks François, 'and the bride and bridegroom never stay with their parents'.

It is rather a surprise to find that according to François 'dancing ranks very low in the pleasures of the English, who generally speaking have no taste for this form of amusement'. He adds that both sexes 'dance equally badly without the least grace or step or rhythm'. One great disadvantage he found in the assembly halls was the custom of never changing partners so that you might be saddled with an uncongenial partner for the whole evening. However, he did himself enjoy dancing in England for two good reasons. He was always complimented on his good performance, whilst in France he was considered rather a bad dancer, and secondly he was able to meet at balls such a great number of new people.

François's diary for his father's reading is also occupied with the love the British have for sport, particularly betting on horses. It sounds distinctly more dangerous than today, as apparently 'a horse very rarely falls. When this does happen the jockey is hurled about 50 feet beyond the horse being also very badly injured . . . ', But according to what I was told, such an accident does not often occur'. All the bets says François, were made by word of mouth, never on paper. There was, it seems, a particular class of racegoer called 'black-legs', who always wore top boots being unable to afford stockings. These men carried their fortunes in their pockets and went from race-course to race-course betting on the horses, laying enormous wagers and mostly growing rich, 'although their fortunes are built only on the somewhat shaky foundations of the chances which their ingenuity contrives to discover'. Apparently the successful 'black-legs' eventually retired from gambling and 'lived like respectable folk' at least. François wrote many pages on horse-racing but not a word does he say about gambling himself. Perhaps the good Pole, Maximilien de Lazowski, kept his charges away from the betting fraternities.

In 1784 François de la Rochefoucauld wrote from what was bitter experience. 'Is there in the world anything so wearisome as the English Sunday? If working days are gloomy, they are festal days by comparison with Sunday'. A young Frenchman could not understand this gloom on a day when every other country as far as he knew made Sunday a day of gaiety and enjoyment. He was amazed to find no singing, except hymns, no playing the piano or other instruments, no dancing and of course certainly no playing cards, ball games, skittles or anything else; not even horse riding was permitted. He assured his father that he dreaded Sundays. Anybody seeing anybody else evading the law was expected to inform the authorities, with the incentive of a reward. Sabbath-breakers could be fined or sent to prison. François added that the highest in the land to the humblest cottager were subject to this law.

Well, then what *do* they do on Sundays in England? One curious omission to Sunday pleasures was drinking. The taverns did a roaring trade where men might easily spend their week's earnings on drink. The women just drank tea, went for walks and gossiped together. The children, he might have added, played with their Noah's Arks.

Naturally, with his father so interested in agriculture, François put a good deal of information in his diary about farms, cattle and other livestock, farm wages, vegetables and rotation of crops. He, his brother and Maximilien, the Polish tutor, all went round Suffolk with Mr Arthur Young and François studiously noted all that he thought would interest his father. Indeed it is quite remarkable to find this young man of barely 19 years old taking such an interest in what he might have been excused from thinking a fairly tedious subject. But no doubt his father had made his own passion interesting to his sons. Certainly François gives no sign of not enjoying the tours round farms of all sizes and kinds. Remembering that the diary was written strictly for his father perhaps it is not so surprising to find so little childish high spirits and gossip in it. However, he does occasionally allow himself a wistful glance in the direction of his contemporaries. For instance, that Mayoral dinner, ball and supper at Lynn must have been a disappointment. There were tables for the two Mayors where all the men sat; another for the two Mayoresses and the ladies and in a separate room sat all the unmarried young men and women. 'Although our place would more naturally have been with these innocents', wrote François, 'the Mayors, by way of doing honour to strangers, invited us to their table. I sat next to Lord Orford'. This laconic utterance surely tells us that his lordship was not interested in the young Frenchman.

When they were at Bury they stayed with a wealthy Scotsman called Mr More, which visit afforded little pleasure to François. 'Mr More's house is not very lively, though there are some young people in it. His daughter and sons did not seem to me to care much for laughter'. Going to visit kind Mr Symonds was pleasanter, but alas the Tuesday receptions, when it was open house for anyone to come for tea and cards, were conducted 'with a touch of solemnity' so that after the second or third Tuesday nobody but old ladies came and no young people at all. 'What could one do in an assembly of serious and wrinkled countenances', complained poor François, 'people entitled by their age to regard themselves as superior to me people who, whether by a kind of natural disdain or by habit and dislike of conversation, never said anything worth saying? Such were our pleasures during a period of eight months'. Nevertheless he must have met a lot of young people earlier on, as we have seen, and formed a good opinion of them.

On his return to Paris he reached the age of twenty-one and passes outside the scope of this book. He certainly made use of his time in England to learn about the ways and customs of our country and he was luckier than James Boswell had been in his Grand Tour of Europe about twenty years earlier, who wrote from Hanover: 'Thus was I laid. In the middle of a great room, upon straw spread on the floor. On the straw was a sheet: I had another sheet as a coverlet. On one side of me were eight or ten horses; on the other four or five cows. A little way from me sat on high a cock and many hens; and before I went to sleep the cock made my ears ring with his shrill voice'.

In 1808 Thomas Cook was born in Derbyshire and this auspicious incident of Georgian days effectively led the way to the eclipse of the Grand Tour in favour of tours for the masses. The inspiration that led to organised travel flashed into the mind of the Baptist preacher-cum-gardener, pedlar and book salesman on his way to Leicester, one day in 1841. He was going to a temperance meeting and it occurred to him how beneficial to all concerned it would be if the railways could be persuaded to run special trains for special occasions. For a shilling apiece no less than 570 intrepid tourists squeezed themselves into the confines of the excessively uncomfortable third-class open carriages and went eleven miles to Loughborough from Leicester and back again at the next delegate meeting of the temperance enthusiasts. By 1855 people were being herded in groups across the Channel and, as an example of the kind of travel they would have encountered, Richard Doyle's amusing book, published in the 1860s will serve as well as any other.

Doyle's illustrations in *Punch* and elsewhere are still sought after by collectors. This large illustrated book, called *The Foreign Tour of Messrs. Brown, Jones and Robinson*, is a sort of missing link between the aristocratic Grand Tour and the Cook's Tour for everybody.

Setting off in a horse-drawn cab to the station, the three young men catch the mail train to Dover which is intolerably crammed with struggling passengers. The luggage is all loaded on to the flat roofs of the carriages. The guard, in a top hat, rings what looks like an enormous dinner-bell regardless of the free-for-all tussling for a place which is going on all round him. That old lady with a parrot in a cage will surely never find a place before the train puffs out of the station.

Our three students are off to Ostend, to tour Belgium, Germany, Switzerland and Italy, and after a rough passage they arrive at Ostend and a fresh conflict with luggage and fellow travellers takes place, exacerbated by the difficulties of foreign ways and language. At the *douane*, Brown finds he has left the key of his bag behind. A picture of the three of them slumbering uncomfortably in a carriage illustrates all that they saw of Belgium. Arrived at Cologne, they suffered the ordeal of the custom's examination, followed by a painful jogging about in a coach to their hotel, once more being packed in like sardines. The 'Speise-saal' hotel is even more full of people than the stations, the trains and the coaches. The bill for their meal gives them a hideous shock and they hasten out to 'do'

Cologne Cathedral, in company with crowds of trippers and a few devout natives. Moving on to Bonn they find the same surges of humanity and face the same exertions with their luggage. Jones has made do with one compact little suitcase, whereas Robinson has brought along enough impedimenta to last him for a year's safari.

After this they board a boat on the Rhine and Brown makes a few sketches of the scenery and of 'heads of the natives'. Their fellow travellers include a tutor and three young gentlemen, his pupils, as well as several other university students and various middle-aged tourists, including intelligent young Americans, quiet happy-faced nuns, smoky young Germans with long beards and longer pipes and a British nobleman. The British ladies are all hidden anonymously behind their bonnets. A meal consumed in the bowels of the steamer, cheek by jowl with all those assorted travellers, must have been a considerable ordeal.

At Coblentz, the sight of a tiny basin suspended on a tiny trivet, which is the entire washing facilities for Brown, Jones and Robinson in their hotel bedrooms, causes Robinson to ring the bell with such violence that all the waiters rush in thinking that either the hotel is on fire or that a revolution has broken out.

Most surprisingly, Jones has brought along his dog and at Coblentz this animal steals a sausage. The whole population rise like one man and hunt him through the town. However, the dog eats the sausage, having outstripped his pursuers, and moreover he takes a bite out of a burly burgher's leg, the man having had the temerity to approach too near.

They go on through Frankfurt and Heidelberg, philosophising amongst the ruins and drinking with local students; Jones's miserable dog causes more trouble at Baden, attacking a sentry this time, and an officer subsequently follows up this occurrence by presenting himself at their hotel, when Jones is arrested and marched off. Robinson feverishly sets off to see His Excellency the British Minister, who manages to liberate Jones and his dog and advises the young man to leave the country as soon and as quietly as possible.

On they go to Basle, Lucerne and over the St Gotthard Pass by a most dangerous looking horse-drawn *diligence*, just as full of passengers as were all their other conveyances. Once in Italy they explore the Italian lakes and mountains and are besieged by beggars in a lonely place. Beggars once more assail them in a Milan cafe and later on they visit a marionette theatre and see a tourist writing his name on the roof of Milan cathedral. Language difficulties beset them in Croatia, and Brown's sketches of the populace cause him to be arrested and taken to the Governor, who, by the mercy of providence, turns out to be Field Marshal Lieutenant Count Brown, a long lost uncle.

On they press to Venice and pass there an excessively long night at the Theatre, which begins at 5 pm and does not finish until 7 o'clock in the morning. The audience is chiefly composed of 'the people' who are in a continual state of extraordinary excitement, fizzing like the perpetual going off of soda-water. The theatre, by the way, is lit dangerously by four oil lamps. The thing that impresses the three young men most unfavourably is the enormous mosquitoes in their bedroom. They do go to the Accademia in Venice to see the pictures, mainly for Brown's benefit, but no mention is made of the famous architecture or other landmarks in any places they visit.

In Vienna they go to the theatre and picture galleries, and also to the Opera. Their visit to Prague is brief as they are now so exhausted with all this rapid travelling and frequent interruptions of their sleep by demands to see their passports, that the homeward journey through the Rhineland again and then through Belgium passes like a dream.

Robinson has bought a few souvenirs of their tour. He is bringing home some eau de Cologne; a pipe, which he will never smoke; a hat, which he never wore and finds a nuisance; some cigars, which the customs officials confiscate; a book, published by a pirate firm called Tauchnitz, which is also confiscated; a *cornet à pistons,* which he hopes some day to learn how to play; and finally gloves, purchased at Venice as a great bargain and now found to be worthless.

They cross the Channel and are inevitably all three very sea-sick and tired out but delighted to be home. They toast each other in a glass of good old English beer—not forgetting the dog.

Well, that tour must have been typical of these of the average Victorian traveller in foreign parts, as opposed to tours of the intellectual and highly educated people who went on the Grand Tour to learn about art and architecture, music and museums, as well as trying to pick up any languages they were not already versed in. Perhaps it was the difference between an education and an experience. Certainly the three young students must have extracted a considerable amount of amusement and interest out of their tour, if precious little uplift. It all depends what you have gone *for*; culture or just seeing how other people live. Nowadays there is very little difference between one country and another, but even in the 1860s there was enough diversity to spice the journey and make it worth while to face all the rigours of mass travel.

Before 1800 of course, when the Grand Tours were in full swing, there were few roads worthy of the name. They were more like tracks than highways, deep rutted and uneven. The very first mail coach in England ran in 1784. Thirteen years later there were no less than 42 routes. From then onwards communications spread rapidly. Today we live in an age of speed and hurry. We are distracted by the wireless and the press and the television. We all of us become increasingly irritable, because quiet and peace are so hard to find. Yet still we travel, mostly in groups for the sake of our shrinking purses.

Our children are used to the noise and bustle and hardly look up at an aeroplane, nor wonder at the astonishing travel of American space-ships to the moon. What sort of tours will they undertake when they grow up? The future belongs, as it always has, to children and it is to them that we look to alter things and to improve them.

Bibliography

SOME BOOKS CONSULTED

LARK RISE TO CANDLEFORD, Flora Thompson, 1939
KILVERT'S DIARY (1870–1879), ed. William Plomer, 1944
MAYHEW'S LONDON, ed. Peter Quennell, 1949
THE LETTERS OF MOZART AND HIS FAMILY, Trans. &
    Ed. Emily Anderson, 1938
MOZART AND HIS WORLD, Erich Valentin, Trans. Margaret
    Shenfield, 1959
THE VICTORIAN AGE, D. C. Somervell, M.A., Published by
    The Historical Association, 1937
TOYS, Patrick Marray, 1968
THE GEORGIANS AT HOME, Elizabeth Burton, 1967
THE VICTORIAN HOUSEHOLD, Marion Lockhead, 1964
THE LIFE OF CHARLOTTE BRONTË, Mrs Gaskell, 1870
LIFE OF JOHNSON, Boswell, ed. Roger Ingpen, 1925
    Jane Austen's Novels
    Brontës' Novels
    Charles Dickens' Novels
    Early Journals of Fanny Burney
THE GRAND TOUR IN THE EIGHTEENTH CENTURY,
    W. E. Mead, 1914
Evelyn's Diary & Correspondence, ed. W. Bray, 1850
Pepys' Diary, Wheatley & Braybrook edition, 1903–4
PRINCES IN THE MAKING, Morris Marples, 1965
HANOVER TO WINDSOR, Roger Fulford, 1960
HINTS TOWARDS FORMING THE CHARACTER OF A
    YOUNG PRINCESS, Hannah More, 1805
QUEEN VICTORIA'S EARLY LETTERS, ed. J. Raymond,
    1963
DAUGHTERS OF GEORGE III, D. M. Stuart, 1939
    Miss Weeton's JOURNAL OF A GOVERNESS (2 Volumes),
    first published 1936 (reprint 1969)
THE OXFORD COMPANION TO THE THEATRE, Hartnell,
    1967
QUEEN ADELAIDE, Mary Hopkirk, 1946
THE CREEVEY PAPERS, ed. Sir Herbert Maxwell, 1904

MÉLANGES SUR L'ANGLETERRE, OR A FRENCHMAN IN ENGLAND, by François de la Rochefoucauld. ed. from MSS by Jean Marchand; trans. & notes, S. C. Roberts Memoirs of the Comtesse de Boigne

THE BOY THROUGH THE AGES, D. M. Stuart, 1926

THE FIRST TEN YEARS, Mario Lockhead, 1956

THE FOREIGN TOUR OF MESSRS. BROWN, JONES AND ROBINSON, Richard Doyle, c 1867

JOURNALS, LETTERS AND VERSES OF MARJORY FLEMING, ed. by Arundell Esdaile

THE COMPLETE MARJORY FLEMING, ed. Frank Sidgwick, 1934

ENGLISH GIRLHOOD AT SCHOOL, D. Gardiner, 1929

A GALAXY OF GOVERNESSES, Bea Howe, 1954

MARIA EDGEWORTH, Isabel Clarke, 1950

EDWARD LEAR, Angus Davidson, 1938

FAMILY LIFE, Christina Hole, 1948

THE TOWER MENAGERIE, Edward Turner Bennett, 1829

THE GRAND WHIGGERY, Marjorie Villiers, 1939

THRALIANA, Extracts from, by C. Hughes, 1913

THE GOVERNESS, OR THE LITTLE FEMALE ACADEMY, Sarah Fielding, 1749

HANNAH MORE AND HER CIRCLE, Mary Alden Hopkins, 1947

MRS. THRALE OF STREATHAM, C. E. Vulliamy, 1936

THE QUEENEY LETTERS, ed. by Lord Lansdowne, 1934

LIFE OF SIR WILLIAM ROWAN HAMILTON, by Robert Perceval Graves, 1882